ADVANCE PRAISE

"*Race to Innovation* is more than a book about business, it's a call to action. At a time when America faces a growing innovation deficit, this powerful work challenges us to confront the systemic barriers that keep too many people, especially Black entrepreneurs, locked out of opportunity. Let this book inspire you to think differently, lead boldly, and invest in the brilliance that exists in every corner of our society."

—**WILLIAM HEATH**, Former Group VP at Eli Lilly and Chief Scientific Officer at Persephoni BioPartners

"Passion for innovation and equity shines through in *Race to Innovation*. I found it both eye-opening and affirming—a reminder that if we want real impact, we must back overlooked innovators with more than words. I'm proud to support this important message."

—**SIMONE GRAPINI-GOODMAN**, Chief Marketing Officer, American Diabetes Association

"In an era marked by unprecedented global and technological transformation, the imperative to translate the best ideas into action swiftly has never been greater. Yet, one of the most underappreciated catalysts of breakthrough innovation is diversity—particularly its role in enabling non-linear, cross-disciplinary thinking. This timely and insightful book offers a critical contribution to our understanding of how diverse perspectives drive meaningful progress in healthcare innovation and beyond. I am honored to endorse its message."

—**RENARD CHARITY**, Growth Strategy Advisor to leading healthcare innovators and Managing Partner at Fletcher Spaght, Inc.

"We are standing at the edge of a new epoch—where innovation is no longer confined to labs or lecture halls but is becoming a dynamic, interconnected ecosystem that shapes every facet of our lives. This is more than a transition; it is a convergence of exponential technologies, reimagined education, and the urgent demands of a rapidly changing world. The global challenges we face—whether in energy, AI governance, or breakthroughs in biotechnology—require a new generation of scientists, systems thinkers, and creative problem-solvers. This realization has deepened my conviction that innovation is not just a discipline—it is the foundation of the future. To meet the moment, we must reimagine how innovation is taught, scaled, and shared, developing agile, tech-enabled, and forward-looking approaches that anticipate and adapt to the needs of the next two decades."

—NAKIA MELECIO, PhD, Senior Research Faculty, Georgia Institute of Technology and Director of National Science Foundation I-Corps Southeast Hub

"*Race to Innovation* is a clear, inspiring look at how smart ideas and teamwork can spark innovation and entrepreneurship in communities often missed. It's a great read for anyone who cares about making progress that matters."

—KATHLEEN SEBELIUS, Former US Secretary of Health and Human Services

"*Race to Innovation* is a timely and insightful exploration of how diversity, resilience, and bold thinking drive true progress. This book challenges conventional norms and offers a powerful road map for leaders, entrepreneurs, and changemakers who want to create lasting impact in today's rapidly evolving world. It's not just a call to innovate—it's a call to lead with intention and purpose. A must-read for anyone serious about shaping the future."

—JOEL WIGGINS, Founder of Wiggins Institute of Entrepreneurship and Life Development

"*Race to Innovation* is a compelling exploration of how entrepreneurship can be a powerful catalyst for economic equity and societal transformation. It acknowledges the hidden history of Black entrepreneurship and systemic barriers to success in America. Bamforth and Zwahlen expertly blend historical context with modern strategies, revealing the untapped potential of Black innovators as drivers of progress. This book is a call to action for leaders to rethink how they invest in diverse talent and ideas—not just as a moral imperative, but as a powerful engine for growth."

—DANIELLE NEVELES-MCGRATH, Chief Impact Officer, Humana Foundation

"This book captures the themes of innovation through stories of grit that show entrepreneurship is not just about money, but also about courage. The free market is the best 'even playing field' we have, and *Race to Innovation* makes clear that our opportunity is to look for and invest in the entrepreneurial spirit in founders of all types. If we do, all our communities benefit from new, innovative, successful enterprises. Read this book!"

—MARCUS WHITNEY, Founder and Managing Partner, Jumpstart Nova

"*Race to Innovation* moved me deeply. It is a story of passion and purpose weaved together to honor the dreams, the grit, and the genius of Black entrepreneurs—many like the ones I grew up with—whose stories are too often overlooked or merely untold. It challenges us to reimagine what's possible when access and opportunity intersect. As an educator and entrepreneur, I found it both emotionally powerful and intellectually necessary."

—BERNARD BELL, Executive Director of the Shuford Program in Entrepreneurship

"*Race to Innovation* provides a unique view into how, in history as well as current times, differences in culture, race, and experiences often produce tremendous value. The concepts the authors share, along with the proof points throughout the many real examples, make a compelling case for why we must all embrace the power of diversity. This book proves that when done right, diversity is clearly a catalyst for success."

—**TONY EZELL**, EVP and President of the Americas, BD

"This book is a vital guide for anyone working to transform opportunity into commercial success—and it makes one thing clear: Diversity isn't optional; it's a strategic advantage. Drawing from deep experience across startups, academia, and industry, *Race to Innovation* illustrates how inclusive participation fuels stronger ideas, broader market relevance, and better outcomes. It's a pragmatic, no-nonsense playbook for building innovation pipelines that reflect the full spectrum of talent and lived experience. If you care about unleashing innovation, you should care about who gets to innovate."

—**DOUG SPEIGHT**, Chief Executive Officer of AxNano, Inc. and Co-Founder of Alcom Capital Partners, LLC

RACE TO INNOVATION

RACE TO INNOVATION

UNLEASHING THE POWER OF ENTREPRENEURSHIP FOR EVERYONE

JOHN BAMFORTH AND **ROY ZWAHLEN**

WITH **REUBEN BLACKWELL, MAYA FITZGERALD,** AND **ASHLIE THOMAS**

IDEAPRESS
PUBLISHING

WASHINGTON, DC

IDEAPRESS
PUBLISHING

Copyright © 2025 by John Bamforth and Roy Zwahlen

All rights reserved. No part of this book may be reproduced, stored, or transmitted by any means—whether auditory, graphic, mechanical, or electronic—without written permission of both publisher and author, except in the case of brief excerpts used in critical articles and reviews. Unauthorized reproduction of any part of this work is illegal and is punishable by law.

Ideapress Publishing | www.ideapresspublishing.com

All trademarks are the property of their respective companies.

Cover Design: Jordan Moss
Interior Design: Jessica Angerstein

Cataloging-in-Publication Data is on file with the Library of Congress.

Hardcover ISBN: 978-1-64687-185-8
eBook ISBN: 978-1-64687-203-9

Special Sales
Ideapress books are available at a special discount for bulk purchases for sales promotions and premiums, or for use in corporate training programs. Special editions, including personalized covers, a custom foreword, corporate imprints, and bonus content, are also available.

1 2 3 4 5 6 7 8 9 10

CONTENTS

- **1**   **INTRODUCTION**   Innovation in Black and White
- **17**   **CHAPTER 1**   America's Hidden History of Innovation and Entrepreneurialism
- **45**   **CHAPTER 2**   It Takes an Enclave
- **65**   **CHAPTER 3**   The Enclave of Education
- **93**   **CHAPTER 4**   The Ownership Imperative
- **113**   **CHAPTER 5**   Empowering Each Unique Lens
- **135**   **CHAPTER 6**   Accelerating Transformative Change by Supporting Innovation
- **157**   **CHAPTER 7**   An Opportunity to Stimulate Innovation in Corporate America
- **171**   **CHAPTER 8**   Expanding the Innovation Zone
- **199**   Acknowledgments
- **201**   Endnotes
- **211**   Index

CONTRIBUTORS

Maya Fitzgerald is a doctor of pharmacy and MBA candidate at the UNC Eshelman School of Pharmacy and UNC Kenan-Flagler Business School. She made major research contributions early in the life of this book. Maya is especially passionate about advancing novel treatments for rare diseases and improving healthcare access, equity, and outcomes through interdisciplinary approaches.

Reuben C. Blackwell, IV, is a leading figure in human services delivery innovation in North Carolina, currently at the helm of Opportunities Industrialization Center of Rocky Mount as CEO. His dedication to empowering underserved and underrepresented communities is at the core of his mission, with a focus on tackling urgent labor shortages and health challenges through innovative social entrepreneurship. Reuben is passionate about ensuring that workers can secure stable, well-paying careers and are operating in the healthiest environments possible. Renowned for his expertise in workforce development strategies, health programming, and leadership development, he leads educational initiatives aimed at strengthening the sustainability and effectiveness of community service organizations.

**Ashlie Thomas** is a social entrepreneur, advocate, and doctoral student at the UNC Gillings School of Global Public Health with a mission to strengthen food systems and improve community health across North Carolina. Her work focuses on advancing nutrition innovation and agricultural education through practical, community-based solutions that address food insecurity and health disparities, particularly in rural and underserved communities. Recognized for her ability to turn research into action, she is dedicated to reshaping food and health systems that reflect the values and needs of the communities they serve.

Introduction

INNOVATION IN BLACK AND WHITE

In 2015, a photograph of a dress went viral on the internet and became an amusing topic of confusion, debate, and curiosity. To some, the dress appeared black and blue. To others, it looked white and gold. The differences were so stark and widespread, it raised questions about the perception of reality itself. Scientists struggled to explain the neuroscientific causes of the confusion. Philosophers weighed in. Hashtags blew up.

Today, that disagreement seems impossibly quaint. We live in a time when political debates have become so fierce and entrenched that they seem to reflect entirely different realities. In a book about entrepreneurialism and innovation—such as this one, designed to steer away from politics and policy—it's become impossible to ignore the political dimensions of our topic. The research, interviews, and writing for this book began in the year after George Floyd's murder, as a surge of heightened awareness about institutional racism led American business leaders and investors to make declarations of support for new programs and efforts to right historic wrongs. That wave today feels as though it has reversed direction with a surge of arguments, legislation, court rulings, policies, and coordinated actions countering the view that race remains a significant factor in today's America and needs to be addressed.

This book may intensify such debates because it presents a perspective of American reality—historical and current—that may be at odds with some views. But the hope is that the ideas and pragmatic solutions we present will resonate across political lines because they can lead to better lives for all Americans.

The broader focus of this book illuminates the virtues of innovation and entrepreneurship, but the deeper argument it makes is that America suffers from an immense innovation deficit that impedes more growth and broader prosperity. Specifically, many marginalized groups of people are restrained from participating fully in the innovation economy—to the detriment of us all.

Black-led entrepreneurialism and innovation then becomes the particular focus, but instead of emphasizing the historical and systemic forces that have held back, oppressed, and even violently fought the efforts of Black entrepreneurs, this book highlights the historic successes and present-day achievements that may be underappreciated or unknown to the general public. And true to its intent, we do not overtly make an argument for political or social solutions. Instead, we advocate for the potential of American innovation and entrepreneurship to find grassroots solutions and transform the very inequities the system perpetuates.

In the end, by offering its relatively unique perspective, this can perhaps be one of many resources to challenge and change the reality of America today, for the benefit of all.

The Innovation Deficit

For many people, America is the land of opportunity. Much of that opportunity has been ascribed to America's broad support for innovation and its openness to change, and to an economic system that abundantly rewards those whose ideas and determination succeed in the marketplace. Proof of that innovative spirit is easy to call up. America has 375 Nobel Prize winners, more than twice the next closest nation. American companies account for 65 percent of the total market value of the world's top 100 companies.[1] America had over 65,000 startups in 2021; while the next highest-ranked country, India, had only 8,300.[2] America has more than twice as many startup unicorns (400 startups valued over $1 billion) as China (158), the second-place country.[3]

This level of success is rightly admired and praised. Yet America lags dramatically on other critical and striking measures of social well-being. On the Legatum Prosperity Index, America ranks 18th out of 167 nations and 59th for health.[4] One of the reasons for that poor showing is that prosperity in America is so uneven, both geographically and in terms of race. Massachusetts, for example, is the most prosperous state in the country, while Mississippi, the least prosperous state, lags far behind economically, educationally, and in terms of health, justice, and democratic representation. Such disparities are striking even within narrower zones. Average life expectancy in parts of Chicago can be 30 years higher than in neighborhoods a ZIP code away.[5] Life expectancy for Black men nationally is 5 years lower than for White men.[6] Median income for middle-class White families in 2016 was $65,041; for Black families it was $39,490.[7] The categories and comparisons go on and on.

Some view the disparity in the American socioeconomic system as a virtue, not a failing; a feature, not a bug. They believe that disparity motivates social striving and catalyzes economic opportunity, that it ultimately propels people and communities toward greater prosperity. The theoretical validity of such a view is debatable, but even if it were true under perfect conditions, the reality of racial disparities—around economics, criminal prosecution, wealth, political power, regulations, housing, transportation, childcare, community resources, political power, health, education, and so on—historically and today—mean that conditions are very imperfect indeed. It's important to state from the outset, however, that racial factors underpin many of the social and economic disparities America faces.

These disparities have a cascading effect, impeding Black entrepreneurs, Black employees, and Black communities from participating fully in the American innovation economy. Compared to their White male counterparts, Black entrepreneurs and Black businesses are under-capitalized, under-resourced, and insufficiently supported. Logically, if 14 percent of the population of the United States faces significant obstacles in pursuing innovation opportunities, discovering and serving market needs, and growing generational wealth, the entire nation is many times poorer as a result.

The solution is not and should not be a paternalistic or White savior approach to rectifying this disparity by "helping" Black people create Black products for Black communities. Instead, it lies in unleashing and proliferating real opportunities so that marginalized people of any race or region can position themselves to develop and deliver innovations for us all. A new wave of American innovation and wealth creation can be unlocked by supporting entrepreneurs from marginalized communities—Black, Somali, Hmong, Appalachian, rural Midwestern, and others—with the resources and capital they need to get into the game. All of us would benefit from the resulting economic growth.

Traditional efforts to improve equity, inclusion, and opportunity usually rely on policy measures, social movements, and improvements to social services, education, or health. All such efforts may be worthy, necessary, and laudable, but they are not always sustainable. Resources run dry. Political winds turn. Backlashes form. Programs may lack the flexibility to adapt to evolving circumstances.

Entrepreneurship and innovation lead to generational wealth and can create more lasting social change. Generational wealth means families have more resources, connections, and power. It also has a compounding effect on resources available for social needs. Higher tax bases mean schools and education programs are better funded. Improved living standards mean better nutrition and health, less stress on the family, and more access to basic resources like computers, Wi-Fi, tutoring, out-of-state colleges, and more. Economic success of this kind (whether driven by successful entrepreneurial ventures or other businesses) breeds more success in a virtuous cycle of economic growth and opportunity expansion. The innovation economy needs to be far more inclusive and diverse, but the basic mechanics of capitalism work.

For marginalized groups in general, and Black Americans in particular, market innovation can be a powerful, game-changing force for catalyzing wealth generation, accelerating the development of economic skills and capabilities, driving economic growth and community prosperity, and improving social equity, while meeting underserved market and societal needs. This book aims to analyze the formula for innovation and how Black entrepreneurs and business leaders succeed despite very real barriers and disparities. Interestingly, this book's interviews with Black founders, investors, and leaders reveal a shared philosophy. They frequently expressed a deep love of community and a personal sense of mission that looms large and permeates their businesses. In many ways, they're in business to support and strengthen the people around them intentionally and by design.

The Innovation Solution

Innovation can take place on many fronts. At the neighborhood level, there is storefront entrepreneurship. With sufficient resources, an individual entrepreneur might buy a franchise or open a business, and thereby grow their personal wealth and improve the prosperity of a community. But few such businesses are scalable and create the kind of wealth that's truly transformational for individuals or communities. This book will explore innovation and entrepreneurship that fills larger or broader market needs. Usually, such innovations rely on technology and global scalability.

This book also explores innovation that is facilitated by improving the level of diversity, equity, and inclusion within boards, executive teams, and the employee base of large established businesses. Such diversity fosters innovation and prosperity because it enables organizations to better discover and meet market needs that are currently underserved. Similarly, enhanced diversity is an important companion to entrepreneurialism because it grows the talent and leadership pool, and gives future leaders and entrepreneurs more opportunities for professional growth, connections, support, know-how, and so on. In an entrepreneur's journey, experience gained in an established business can be an important seeding ground for innovations they eventually bring to market.

This book acknowledges the institutional and systemic barriers that have impeded Black entrepreneurialism and innovation historically and today, just as it uncovers its hidden history and a few of its remarkable successes.

Within all of this lies a practical path to wealth generation for individuals, businesses, and communities from underrepresented groups.

INTRODUCTION

Our chapters follow that path, marked by five road signs:

1. **Recognize Potential**—Entrepreneurship and innovation are premised on the discovery of underappreciated, overlooked market opportunities. Marginalized entrepreneurs, communities, and market needs represent potential with outsized return on investment opportunities. This is reflected in the hidden history and powerful presence of Black entrepreneurship. See Chapter 1, "America's Hidden History of Innovation and Entrepreneurialism."

2. **Power of Enclaves**—Every entrepreneur's journey is hard, but mainstream entrepreneurs benefit from social and psychological support, networks and connections, and an unwritten playbook for success that minority entrepreneurs do not have ready access to. Enclaves, including neighborhoods, friends and family, churches, colleges (especially HBCUs), networking groups, and supportive investment funds, are more valuable than most realize and create preconditions for later success. See Chapter 2, "It Takes an Enclave," and Chapter 3, "The Enclave of Education."

3. **Enable Ownership**—The premise of wealth generation is ownership. Well-paying corporate and professional positions may be less risky and more socially acceptable (especially for first-generation college graduates), and can lead to individual and family prosperity, but they will not likely produce game-changing wealth. Only ownership does that, as even Michael Jordan can attest. See Chapter 4, "The Ownership Imperative."

4. **Unique Lens**—Back to those overlooked, underserved market needs: Diverse entrepreneurs and innovators have a unique lens on such opportunities. And, often, their ideas are scalable to larger markets. See Chapter 5, "Empowering Each Unique Lens."

5. **Accelerate Transformative Change**—Every startup and innovation benefits from fuel applied to the fire at the right time. This can

come from connections, pilots, investment, mentorship, a complementary team, partnerships, boot camps, accelerators, and venture studios. The goal is to seize opportunities, grow, and build value at an accelerated pace. And that speeds up the impact on markets and communities, too. See Chapter 6, "Accelerating Transformative Change by Supporting Innovation."

Many of these concepts can be explored in a corporate setting. Chapter 7 features interviews conducted with former leaders at Eli Lilly and Company. Their insights highlighted the company's effort to research and report on the lived experience of all employees from disparate backgrounds. Lilly leadership believed that this focus on engaging all employees would benefit innovation and performance across the enterprise. It is hard, perhaps, to directly correlate these efforts to the company's returns. However, Lilly is now viewed by many as one of the most innovative pharmaceutical companies in the world, and excellent financial performance followed.

Finally, Chapter 8, "Expanding the Innovation Zone," explores how the principles shared throughout the book apply beyond the Black community to all communities.

Along the way, this book will:
- Examine the societal, organizational, and economic barriers to Black entrepreneurship and greater organizational diversity.
- Detail the economic and societal consequences of America's innovation deficit and lay out the benefits that become possible when that deficit is overcome.
- Illustrate the benefits of innovation and entrepreneurialism as grassroots approaches to meeting market needs and solving societal gaps.
- Dig into solutions to those barriers and describe how entrepreneurs increase their access to capital, resources, know-how, connections, and markets.

- Reflect on how organizations can meaningfully improve and leverage their diversity through practical programs and approaches.
- Explore scalable market needs that can be uniquely met by Black ventures and businesses, and how those innovations can solve enormous societal and global challenges.

A Note from the Authors

We started this introduction with a discussion of perspective and how different vantage points influence our understanding of reality and may shape it. For that reason, it's important to describe the personal perspectives we bring to this project.

It may be unusual to have two co-authors, but we have found it invaluable at every stage of this process to rely on each other and on our colleagues and networks to share and leverage our collective experiences, surface our assumptions, and debate our solutions.

Who We Are

John Bamforth came of age in the sixties and seventies in the northwest of England. His hometown of Wigan could not have been more White and blue collar. Wigan is an old coal-mining town, forged in the Industrial Revolution, founded on a hard-nosed, straightforward culture brought to life in George Orwell's book *The Road to Wigan Pier* and best personified by its champion rugby team. Growing up, John had no idea how "white" his world was. Most of his encounters with people of color were infused by a level of casual, demeaning, and dehumanizing racism across his community that still shocks him today.

His world opened up, as it does for many, when he went off to college at the University of Bath and later to graduate school at Aston University in Birmingham. He began to make friends with people from an array of backgrounds and developed a deep, lifelong interest in other cultures and subcultures, which has enriched his academic, professional, and personal journey through life.

With a PhD in neuropharmacology, John joined Eli Lilly in 1989, and focused on building global brands and leading highly engaged and diverse teams. He emigrated to the United States in 2001. After retiring from Eli Lilly, he returned to academia to lead Eshelman Innovation at the University of North Carolina, Chapel Hill. This institute focuses on translating the brightest and best ideas on campus into products and services that impact patients.

Roy Zwahlen grew up an army brat. At a time when many career military officers studied Russian, Roy's father studied Arabic. As a result, Roy spent most of his formative years in the Middle East in Jordan, Turkey, Kuwait, and Syria. In this great crossroads of history, civilization, commerce, religion, language, and politics, he was exposed to a diversity of cultures hard to find in other corners of the world.

His educational experience was similarly diverse and unusual. Though taught in American schools abroad, his schools were filled with a mix of local students and the children of diplomats from around the world. His daily exposure to different cultures, languages, ideas, and people shaped his experience of life. His periodic returns to the US were both exciting and disorienting. Extracted from a mosaic of celebrated cultures, he encountered the challenging need to navigate subtle and not-so-subtle racial and ethnic barriers and divisions in schools. While the Middle East was no paradise, he found that his America had a ways to go to live up to the ideals taught to him by his veteran father and veteran grandfathers.

INTRODUCTION

At Brigham Young University, he experienced another kind of disorientation when he became immersed for the first time in his own majority religious culture. While he shared a faith with this community, he did not find much commonality with his life experiences or his global views. This was not unusual for Roy in the United States, just unexpected, and he loved it. He was drawn to the opportunity of multicultural societies found in subjects like political science, economics, and international affairs, studying the history of racism, finance of the Ottoman Empire, and the political history of South Asia. After earning his law degree at George Mason School of Law, he specialized in intellectual property, international trade, public health, and economic development. He spent the first half of his career conducting think-tank activities for the biotech industry and advising state, national, and international bodies. After advising governments and industry on best-in-class technology innovation and entrepreneurism development economic models and policy for biotech, he decided to roll up his sleeves and build a model from the ground up. As the chief strategy officer for Eshelman Innovation, Roy is responsible for building and managing strategy, governance, and operations.

We met in Chapel Hill, North Carolina, at Eshelman Innovation. *Race to Innovation* is a culmination of our work and life experiences in diversity and innovation, the experiences of our diverse colleagues and friends as they've navigated this "land of opportunity," and the innovation and entrepreneurial frameworks we have developed and implemented. The events of the past few years, from the death of George Floyd to the pandemic, have opened our eyes to the complexities pervading our nation's politics and history. Fortunately, our innovation and entrepreneurial mindset have helped us look deeply into problems, listen intently to business and venture leaders, and serve as allies in connecting them to solutions, resources, strategies, and tools that are necessary for their success, if insufficient.

Race to Innovation is both descriptive and prescriptive. It draws upon ongoing research into innovation, entrepreneurialism, American history, race, society, and economics. We rely heavily on our ongoing conversations with people who are confronting barriers to innovation, and who directly understand the challenges and journeys associated with innovating. Some of these people may one day become household names. Most share our view that success in entrepreneurialism and innovation are key to the kind of wealth generation that can transform our societal challenges and solve the innovation deficit. Our perspective is optimistic without being naïve, and our bias is toward practical solutions. We are trained to engineer from need to opportunity and to continually examine the challenges we encounter and the resources at our disposal in ways that hopefully improve or enhance the likelihood of success.

Our focus on the Black experience of entrepreneurialism and innovation does not mean we are indifferent to or ignorant of the challenges faced by other marginalized groups. We believe that each marginalized group has its own history and faces its own challenges in driving innovation. The experiences of Latinx, East Indian, Chinese, and Native American populations, for example, are very different from each other, as are the experiences of women, LGBTQ individuals, and the differently abled. But the basic principles of innovation, markets, and investment capital mean that all groups will arrive at similar solutions to overcoming those barriers. As such, we think that the ideas and strategies we describe in this book for Black entrepreneurs will be helpful and inspiring for other marginalized people.

We're excited to celebrate the successes and accomplishments of Black entrepreneurs and Black-led innovations that don't get the mainstream attention they deserve. We're also keenly aware that America has a long history of reactionary backlash to Black business success and socioeconomic advancement. Politics, policies, rhetoric, social movements, and regulations can be wielded by communities, banks, businesses, chambers of commerce, clubs, and others to impede that success and advancement, sometimes with devastating results. Perhaps those counter-efforts are based on a mistaken view that the economic pie of America is only so large and can't be shared without sacrifice. The truth is that innovation and economic success are not zero-sum games in which participants compete over limited resources and rewards. When innovation and economic activity increases, the pie grows, often dramatically, and everyone benefits. We believe that the forces of innovation can overcome such challenges with the right strategies, resources, networks, and support.

Life, Liberty, and the Pursuit of Ownership

In his rough draft of the Declaration of Independence, Thomas Jefferson penned one of the most profound and even revolutionary sentences in human history:

> *We hold these truths to be sacred & undeniable; that all men are created equal & independent, that from that equal creation they derive rights inherent & inalienable, among which are the preservation of life, & liberty, & the pursuit of happiness.*

It is very likely that Jefferson's inspiration came from liberal philosopher John Locke, who wrote in his "Two Treatises of Government" that society existed to serve the individual's rights to life, liberty, and estate, not the other way round. By *estate*, Locke meant something broader than some manor or splendid piece of property. He was referring to a sense of ownership, not only over land but also over one's body, decisions, and path through life. It's fascinating that Jefferson exchanged that one word, *estate*, for the phrase "pursuit of happiness." In a way, he captured the essence of Locke's intention while giving it an expanded meaning. A sense of self-empowerment is fundamental to the kind of ownership Locke proposed and just as fundamental to a sense of engagement, striving, and purpose, of the kind that Jefferson and his fellow revolutionaries were attempting to capture and instill in their new nation. They wanted nothing short of ownership over their own country, their own lands, their own money, their own lives. They wanted all men (except their slaves, of course) to be free to fail or succeed on their own capabilities and merits.

A satisfying definition of entrepreneurship is hard to wrestle down. In its basic sense, an entrepreneur is someone who starts a business. The risk they take in doing so, investing ideas, expertise, time, energy, reputation, and money—their own and others'—makes them eligible for outsized rewards. But it's the journey itself that makes an entrepreneur. They're in pursuit of something—and it's not always riches or success. Maybe it's happiness, but we don't know many entrepreneurs who arrive at a spot they call happiness and consider the game won. Usually, they jump back in more quickly than they promised themselves and their significant others that they would. Off again, in pursuit of something.

Another thing we say entrepreneurs are often driven by is an idea. They tend to be creative thinkers and innovators. Often, they run on instinct, as artists. They best apply their creativity to practical problem-solving, bringing an analytical sense of the market and need that others are failing to fill.

But, again, there are just as many entrepreneurs who hold no particular passion for the product or service they devote years of their lives to delivering. They're driven by something else.

Money might be the goal, and it's certainly a nice reward. But there are easier ways to make money than entrepreneurship. A good corporate job may come with a much steadier income and a lot less pain and suffering.

In fact, there are countless stories of entrepreneurs who don't get rich, either because their businesses fail or because they don't retain the kind of ownership that their investors secure for themselves. Even if the company pays off, the entrepreneur may only earn a fraction of its value, or none at all. This kind of failure happens all the time.

That is a clue. In our experience and interviews with entrepreneurs, the pursuit of estate or happiness is a longing for ownership, not so much of a company, idea, product, or market, but of one's own labor.

Entrepreneurs are often driven by a desire to not work for others. They may work for a startup or an innovative corporate department because it reinforces their sense of agency, but their fundamental driver is to control or own as much of their labor, effort, creativity, personal investment, and passion as they can.

To fulfill that drive for ownership, entrepreneurs hustle. No entrepreneur starts with everything they need to make their innovation succeed. Most come in with some tangible or intangible assets in hand—an idea that no one else has, expertise, an understanding of how businesses are built and grown, financial resources, supportive families, a great network—but few have all of those things, and many have very little of them. In fact, one of the *a-ha* moments in entrepreneurship comes when you realize that almost every entrepreneur has gaps in their knowledge, experience, understanding, and assets. You are not alone in your deficiencies.

The hustle is a relentless determination to obtain whatever you need to get over the hurdles in front of you, and the many hurdles down the road. In fact, it's impossible to predict what all those hurdles or challenges will be. Too often, entrepreneurs lack some mysterious combination of the necessary traits, capabilities, and assets needed to succeed, and can't get their promising ventures off the ground. Sometimes they're limited by circumstance—a lack of personal or familial resources, education, exposure to opportunity or role models, connections, or access to funders, backers, or potential customers. And sometimes they're also limited by perceptions and biases. Something is certainly lost when that potential is not enabled or realized.

We believe entrepreneurship and innovation are game changers for marginalized American communities, from which everyone benefits, and that support for such entrepreneurs and innovators is a smarter investment with higher potential returns than many realize. We hope that *Race to Innovation* encourages conversation and debate, and that, most importantly, it helps catalyze innovation. As a country, we may not share perspectives as widely as would be ideal, but many of us across different backgrounds and viewpoints share a belief that innovation can improve life and solve problems like no other tool.

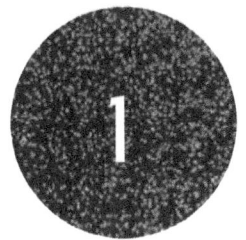

AMERICA'S HIDDEN HISTORY OF INNOVATION AND ENTREPRENEURIALISM

In 2001, co-author John Bamforth emigrated with his family to Indianapolis, Indiana, to work at Eli Lilly's corporate headquarters. It became apparent that, even though he had already worked for the company for 11 years, the Midwest culture was going to be a very new experience. Even though the community was largely welcoming, it took many years before he truly felt part of the city and became more keenly aware of some of Indiana's history, including a building on Indiana Avenue, the Madam C. J. Walker Theater. Driving past the African art deco building intrigued John, but not until many years later did he fully understand the magnitude of what that building represented and the force of nature that was Madam C. J. Walker.

By any measure—her social standing, her lack of education, her economic circumstances, her marriages, her gender, and most of all, her race—she had no chance to achieve so much. Yet Sarah Breedlove, who changed her name to Madam C. J. Walker and launched a beauty products empire that continues to this day, is known as America's first female self-made millionaire, and she was Black.

Her life story is better known today than it was even a few decades ago, thanks to a biography by her granddaughter, a play, a TV show, several documentaries, and many news stories. But how her story challenges assumptions about race, class, gender, and opportunity remains under-examined. The remarkable life of Madam C. J. Walker helps illustrate the potential of innovation, entrepreneurship, and wealth creation to change lives, shift the dynamics of societal power, and lift communities.

Sarah Breedlove was born in 1867, two years after the end of the Civil War and two days before Christmas, near the village of Delta, in northeast Louisiana. She was the first child in her family not to be enslaved at the local plantation. Though born into freedom, her life was hard. She was orphaned by seven, married by 14, and had her first child at 18. Along the way, she received the barest formal education and only learned to read because of Sunday school. As soon as she could, she fled to St. Louis with her new husband to seek economic opportunity in a city where three of her brothers had settled. Her husband died when she was only 20, leaving her more vulnerable than ever. She found work washing laundry, where she made about a dollar a day, and tried to survive as a single mother, while seeing her daughter get the education that she had missed.

There was little about her life over the next decade and a half that would be considered notable or that would lead anyone to predict what she built for herself. She remarried at 27 and divorced her second husband at

36. Her third marriage was to a newspaper advertising salesman in Denver. She was 39 when they married and 45 when they divorced, but she kept her third husband's name, Charles Joseph Walker. Later, when she launched her line of hair products, she called herself Madam C. J. Walker after that husband, who'd also been her business partner.

The innovation, like many business ideas that gain traction, arose out of need, both personal and market-based. Because of poor nutrition and lack of access to clean water and good soap, Sarah Breedlove had dry skin and terrible dandruff, and her hair came out in clumps. To hydrate her skin and preserve her remaining hair, she experimented with various products, some of them homemade solutions.

In this effort, she had some social and familial support. Her St. Louis–based brothers were barbers and well-connected to salespeople who specialized in products that suited the distinct hair and skin needs of Black people. This was a market largely ignored by mainstream manufacturers. However, a Black female entrepreneur named Annie Malone had experienced a lot of success serving those needs. Drawn to the products and intrigued by the business opportunities, Sarah Breedlove became a commissioned saleswoman for Malone, who was 10 years her junior.

Entrepreneurs inspire other entrepreneurs, modeling possibilities that might not even have been imagined before. Their success seeds the economic and social conditions that give rise to wealth, knowledge, connections, entrepreneurialism, and innovation. Without Annie Malone, there likely would never have been a Madam C. J. Walker. Their stories had many similarities. Like Sarah Breedlove, Annie Malone had been born to enslaved parents, was orphaned at a young age, fled economic hardship for opportunity, and became fascinated with hair care. She developed her products for Black women and sold them door-to-door, then moved to St. Louis, a city that was thriving at the time and bursting with economic growth. There, she opened a shop and began to advertise. Later, she launched Poro College, a combination of cosmetology school, manufacturing shop, retail store, and community gathering place that employed hundreds. It's estimated her business ultimately created jobs for 75,000 people around the world. Malone also became a generous donor to causes supporting Black communities.

As a commissioned saleswoman, Breedlove quickly learned a lot from Malone's business savvy and operations, such as how to connect to customers and upsell. She saw how products move and markets grow. She saw that a Black woman entrepreneur could thrive and succeed. Something in Breedlove shifted. Her ambition. Her clarity. Her sense of opportunity. Only a year after starting her new job, she set out for Denver, Colorado, to take on a new territory in Malone's growing empire. It was a big risk for a single mother earning a decent living for the first time, but Denver represented a major new market with significant potential for growth. Sarah Breedlove took a chance.

In Denver, she met Charles Joseph Walker, who shared her passion for sales, promotion, and business. They married and she took his name, becoming Madam C. J. Walker. (The *Madam* was a flourish that gave her an air of French sophistication appropriate for the beauty industry.) Then, the innovation happened. Walker had been experimenting with her hair products for years, well before she joined Malone's business. In Denver, she discovered a formula that was pleasing and effective, and she began to sell it door-to-door. She later said that she received "her hair grower [formula] through a dream." Walker's ambitions for growing her line created a breach with Malone, but Walker and her husband were not dissuaded and went all in on the new product. Walker appointed her daughter as head of her mail-order business. She and her husband then hit the road, traveling around the South and East of the country, developing sales channels, and building her brand. In each new market, Walker typically focused on Black churches, where she knew her audience and potential customers well. They represented a safe space—an enclave, as we'll describe later—for putting herself and her ideas forward.

The business grew rapidly. In 1908, only a few years after launching her new venture, she moved her headquarters to Pittsburgh, where she also opened a college to train licensed saleswomen in Walker beauty products and the Walker system of sales and marketing. Through that training, and some savvy approaches to licensing and commission selling, Walker began to build her empire with many willing followers. Like most successful business leaders today, Walker didn't think of sales as a one-time transaction but as the potential start of an ongoing customer relationship. She trained her expanding sales team (numbering several thousand women by 1917) to teach and provide advice to customers as part of their service offering. Customers saw those salespeople as trusted experts and even friends. This approach facilitated a consistent customer experience. Walker's salespeople grew their commissions, made the company profitable, and expanded the overall revenue stream. The business continued to grow. In 1910, she moved her headquarters to Indianapolis, adding a research laboratory to her school, salon, and factory.

Walker's impact went well beyond her own profitable business and personal success. She changed lives. Several people who worked for her, both men and women, would go on to have distinguished careers of their own. Walker also encouraged the Black women who sold her products to start and manage their businesses. She knew the benefits that financial independence, education, and personal wealth had given her, and understood the impact this could have on improving living conditions and opening doors for members of the Black community. In 1917, she established clubs nationwide for independent businesswomen and convened an annual national conference to bring women together to talk about business, commerce, entrepreneurialism, and charitable giving.

Reaching a level of status and success that few manage, Breedlove moved to Irvington, New York, and bought a mansion that became a center of Black political activism. People who were instrumental in the Harlem Renaissance would meet there to discuss race relations and strategies for social change. Walker also spoke publicly on political, social, and economic issues and was an important leader for the National Association for the Advancement of Colored People. She was also a generous donor to philanthropic causes.

Upon her death at age 51, from complications due to hypertension, she was the wealthiest African American woman in the country. Describing her life journey, she said: "I am a woman who came from the cotton fields of the South. From there, I was promoted to the washtub. From there, I was promoted to the cook kitchen. From there, I promoted myself into the business of manufacturing hair goods and preparations. I have built my factory on my own ground."[1]

The Rise (and Fall) of Black Wall Streets

One of the most amazing aspects of Madam Walker and Annie Malone's stories is that they were not alone. Only a few short years after the Civil War ended, remarkable people who had been raised in enslavement were finding ways to lead new lives and build thriving communities, despite starting with very little and facing enormous barriers to their prosperity.

As newly freed people, African Americans lacked access to the key generators of wealth creation. They had no inherited wealth and did not own land. They could not easily access loans to support businesses or mortgages to buy homes. They faced discriminatory legal and financial practices at every turn. They were paid less than Whites and were resented and attacked for pushing down wages as a result. Many turned to sharecropping out of desperation, a life that was little different from slavery except in name. There were attempts at support—calls to give the formerly enslaved the land they had once forcibly worked, to provide them with 40 acres and a mule, or to establish colonies where they could come together to work their land and own their labor. These calls extended to Congress, which during the Lincoln Administration established the Freedmen's Bureau to help formerly enslaved persons with food, housing, education, healthcare, and employment. Hundreds of Bureau agents dispersed to the Southern states to give support, establish schools, record stories, document injustices, and provide medical care.

Congress also established the Freedman's Bank in 1865 to catalyze Black economic empowerment. The bank offered Blacks, including many who had served in the Union Army, a safe place to put their money and educational programs on how to budget or invest in new businesses. They even offered employment to clerks and cashiers. The need for that support was immense, and the Freedman's Bank branches opened across the Southern states. By 1872, nearly 100,000 Black Americans had accounts with the bank, collectively saving $3.7 million, equal to about $80 million today. But fraud and financial misconduct plagued the bank, and the economic panic of 1873 was a killing blow. Bank runs led to its failure in 1874, wiping out the hard-earned savings of many people, further hindering their opportunities for economic advancement.

The St. Luke's Penny Savings Bank was a different story. It was started by Maggie Lena Walker, who was born in 1864, a few years before Sarah Breedlove, in Richmond, Virginia, the very heart of the Confederacy. Maggie Walker's mother, who had been enslaved herself, worked as a laundress when Maggie was little so the family could survive. Maggie's father had died young. Despite their hard life, Maggie Walker did not lack social support. Her family belonged to a church that was an economic, political, and social center for the Black community. At the age of 14, she joined the Independent Order of St. Luke. This Black fraternal society was instrumental in helping young people develop their independence and self-reliance while ministering to the sick and aged.

In her early twenties, Maggie Walker launched a sister organization focusing on education, community service, and money management while helping enterprising people with resources to start new businesses. She saw the value of that work as a tool for social change and personal improvement, so she decided to take things a step further and opened a bank for Black customers. To prepare for that endeavor, she worked at the White-owned Merchants National Bank of Richmond and studied their processes and how they conducted business.

In 1902, she launched the St. Luke Penny Savings Bank and became its president, the first African American woman to head a bank. She leveraged her relationships within the Black community and the fraternal order councils to encourage people to open accounts and buy bank stock. In 1903, she formally opened the St. Luke Penny Savings with $9,340.44 in deposits and stock purchases. The next year, she convinced the bank's board of directors and the Independent Order of St. Luke to collaborate on the purchase of a building to house a department store (the St. Luke Emporium) and her bank. The bank moved into that location in 1905.

The years that followed were not without challenges. The department store struggled and closed, so the bank erected a new building in 1910. That same year, the Virginia General Assembly passed legislation requiring bank audits that led to the closure of many banks across the state, including the True Reformers Bank, the first Black-owned bank in Richmond. Richmond's Black community lacked confidence in banks due to revelations of unsecured loans, lax operations, and even embezzlement, but the St. Luke Penny Savings Bank weathered the storm.

Competition was another challenge, leading to a merger with two other banks in 1929 and 1930. Walker became chairman of the board of the combined entity, which managed to survive the Great Depression and preserve its independence until 2005, when it was finally acquired. Along the way, the bank made an enormous difference in people's lives. By 1920 alone, the St. Luke Penny Savings Bank had issued more than 600 mortgages to Black families and employed many Black workers.

Aided by such efforts, Black communities began to prosper. Wilmington, North Carolina, quickly became a shining example of that prosperity and, for a time, a model of racial inclusion and collaboration.

Immediately after the Civil War, Black Americans in Wilmington who had been enslaved or were the children of enslaved people used their skills as free people to earn a living. Soon, they accounted for over a third of the labor force in the city. At last, they owned their labor and could benefit from the economic value it created. Many used their service jobs as springboards to other types of employment, earning higher wages and gaining greater opportunities for a secure and prosperous life. They became skilled craftsmen, mechanics, jewelers, plumbers, stevedores, and so on. Slowly and incrementally, they accumulated wealth, stability, social significance, and property. They built businesses, went to school, and opened new horizons. As a population, the Blacks of Wilmington came to prominence and even dominance in many sectors of the economy as owners of barbershops, restaurants, tailoring businesses, and butcher shops. A few people achieved elevated positions. The Manly brothers launched a newspaper. Thomas Miller became a high-profile real estate agent and auctioneer. Frederick Sadgwar was a successful financier and architect.

This growing economic power was matched by increasing social and political power. Blacks composed 55 percent of the population of Wilmington, which was the most populous city in North Carolina at the time. Many now came from an educated middle class. The economic depression of 1892 spurred an interracial partnership between Populists and Black Republicans, known as the Fusion Coalition. The groups shared a belief in self-governance, free public education, and equal voting rights. Blacks got elected to local political positions and served broadly across civic functions. The local government included Black aldermen, postmasters, magistrates, health inspectors, policemen, and a county treasurer.

The increasingly prosperous Black population of Wilmington faced challenges, however. The formerly enslaved and their children had no inherited wealth. Moreover, there was great distrust in financial institutions because of the failure of the Freedmen Bank, which had wiped out the savings of many Black residents of Wilmington. Blacks were also leery of debt because of their history of indebted slavery. Most were unable to get loans or credit at fair interest rates, and were typically forced to pay double the 7.5 percent that Whites without means paid. Lenders even refused to let Blacks pay off their home mortgages in installments, instead requiring a hefty lump sum. These conditions and practices made it difficult to save, invest, and grow wealth, let alone raise a family to gain advantages not afforded to their parents.

Property ownership among Blacks in Wilmington was accordingly rare. Though 60 percent of the region's population, they owned only 8 percent of the property. Since local taxes were primarily based on property, this reduced the amount that Blacks paid relative to Whites, which fostered resentment. Whites criticized the city's Black population for their reduced tax burden, their growing political power and influence, and the competition between Whites and Blacks for skilled-labor jobs.

Those tensions exploded in 1898. That's when White supremacists overthrew the duly elected coalition government, destroyed Black businesses throughout the city, including the nation's only Black newspaper at the time, and killed between 60 and 300 people. Wilmington was not alone. The tragic outcome for its Black population was part of the oppression of Blacks throughout the country as Jim Crow laws renewed racial segregation and made it significantly harder for Blacks to gain education and participate in society and the economy.

Twenty years later, things looked different in the Tulsa, Oklahoma, neighborhood called Greenwood. As in Wilmington, Blacks in Tulsa worked mostly as servants and in low-level service jobs. But the segregation of Blacks from Whites had an unexpected effect. It made the Greenwood neighborhood's economy a "self-contained hub,"[2] and gave it the space and time to grow. As incomes rose, Black businesses and services were born to serve the needs of the community. Those businesses included grocery stores, barbershops, newspapers, schools, physician clinics, architectural firms, and real estate companies.[3] The neighborhood that had been shut off from the rest of the city became known as Black Wall Street because of its prosperity.

The stories of those entrepreneurs and innovators could fill many more books. A former pilot named Simon Berry bought a Model T Ford and launched a taxi service because Black people could not use the Whites-only taxis in Tulsa. Later, he expanded his business to include a bus line and even a charter plane for wealthy oilmen.[4] A lawyer from Kentucky named J. B. Stradford moved to Tulsa and invested in real estate, including pool halls and boarding houses. Eventually he built the luxurious Stradford Hotel, becoming the first Black owner of a hotel in the country. O. W. Gurley, known as the founder of Greenwood, was also drawn to Tulsa because of its wealth. A serial entrepreneur, he established a rooming house, made many real estate investments, and loaned money to other Black residents to start their businesses, helping catalyze the economic dynamism and prosperity of the community.

By 1919, the resurgence of the Ku Klux Klan (KKK) had renewed racial oppression and violence around the country. In Oklahoma, there were organized efforts to disenfranchise Blacks from political power. The Black residents of Tulsa met injustices and incidents of violence with their protests, but White resentment over Black prosperity only grew. Mobs of armed White men advanced on Blacks throughout the city. Blacks retreated to the Greenwood neighborhood for safety, but the marauders overwhelmed the community, burned down its businesses, looted many homes, and murdered an estimated 100–300 Black residents without restraint.[5]

It's estimated that property damage alone amounted to more than $200 million in today's dollars, but the devastation went even deeper. Those armed White men sought to murder Greenwood's spirit and the dream of a prosperous, thriving, safe community for Blacks in an often violent and hostile America. In many ways, for a very long time, they succeeded.

And Rise Again

The story of the destruction of Tulsa's Black Wall Street was relatively unknown until recently when new research, reports, books, and even a fictional depiction in a TV show, *Watchmen*, brought it to light with dramatic intensity. Until then, the event was an open secret, not discussed or commemorated, and out of the public's imagination. Many of the dead had been buried in mass graves, and the truth was buried, too. The massacre was not taught in schools or discussed publicly. The children and grandchildren of Greenwood learned about that history as adults, often in whispers, as something that could not be talked about safely.

Remarkably, the Greenwood community did not completely disappear. Some of the wealthier residents and business owners were able to rebuild their homes and businesses. But Greenwood had lost its dynamism. The trauma of the massacre lived on, affecting relationships, families, decisions, and a sense of belonging. No doubt, those memories made many people more cautious, reluctant, and fearful, dampening their courage, optimism, and confidence. How much economic and human vitality was lost by the people of Greenwood and Tulsa, and the nation as a whole? That city within a city could have been an economic engine for decades, compounding wealth, innovation, education, and opportunity for many generations. Multiply that by all the other Black Wall Streets, communities, and lives affected by systemic and individual racism around the country. The scale of loss is incalculable.

Today, our society memorializes the destruction of those Black Wall Streets but reflects less on the stories of how they were first built and came to prominence. We overlook the resilience, determination, community, optimism, resourcefulness, and creativity that gave rise to such opportunity and prosperity in the first place.

In Durham, North Carolina, another Black Wall Street grew, but this one managed to survive the backlash that destroyed the prospects of generations of Black people in Tulsa and Wilmington, fostering a different trajectory for the city. Once again, Black-owned banks were key to the community's economic growth. One of those bankers was Charles Clinton Spaulding, born in rural North Carolina in 1874. At age 20, Spaulding left his family farm for Durham and became the manager of a Black-owned grocery store. A year later, he started working part time as a salesman for the North Carolina Mutual and Provident Association, a Black-run insurance company that specialized in burial insurance. Soon, Spaulding became a general manager.

Spaulding had notable managerial skills. His nickname was Mr. Cooperation, and he rose quickly through the ranks as the company grew. He became vice president in 1908 and secretary-treasurer in 1919, when the firm's name changed to the North Carolina Mutual Life Insurance Company. In 1923, he was named president.

By then, the company was considered the largest African American business in the world, with assets of over $40 million and a network of subsidiaries. Throughout Spaulding's tenure, which lasted until he died in 1952, the firm established a long track record of supporting Black-owned businesses and Black causes, while promoting economic growth, Black employment, and talent development, which helped foster the rise of a

Black middle class. North Carolina Mutual was also a pioneer in corporate social responsibility. Spaulding wrote an article in 1937 laying out his Four Cardinal Points of Entrepreneurship, one of which was "Social service in business."[6] As he put it, his firm was not only interested in profit, but in ensuring that businesses were socially responsible to the communities they served. The financial institutions he seeded improved living and working conditions for Black Americans and promoted better race relations by fostering collaboration between Blacks and Whites, efforts that W. E. B. Du Bois described as emphasizing cooperation over capitalism. Spaulding also promoted political and educational issues, supported voter registration efforts, and convinced city officials to hire Black police officers. His impact was wide and profound.

Such an environment must have been a draw for many Black Americans seeking economic opportunity and a better life. One of those people was Theodore Roosevelt Speight, who moved from a farm in the Greenville area of eastern North Carolina to Durham in the mid-1930s. Though self-taught and poor, Theodore Speight was handy with electrical and mechanical devices and got a job working for the White owner of a gas station that serviced Model T Fords but did not serve the Black community. Two years later, Theodore left to start his own auto company to do just that. It was a daring venture during the Great Depression in the Jim Crow South. Black entrepreneurs had little access to money from White banks, but Durham's Black Wall Street community was a source of inspiration, support, capital, and equipment. Notably, Theodore's former employer became his first investor and remained a mentor and friend for the rest of his life. Transcending race through collaboration with like-minded innovators and investors would be a running theme for the Speight family over successive generations.

Theodore's auto service business was on the cutting edge of technology and market demand, not unlike a high-tech business today. The vision of bringing auto services to Black consumers proved profitable, and Theodore soon expanded into related businesses like heating oil delivery.

With that success came more opportunities. Theodore's son, Melvin, was able to get the education his father had not been able to attain. Melvin attended North Carolina Agricultural and Technical State University (NC A&T State), where he studied automotive technology. Afterward, he worked with his father, and between the two of them, they founded and owned eight companies in total, building on the success of Speight's Auto Service, which continued to operate for almost a century after its founding.

Growing up in that entrepreneurial family environment, Melvin's son, Doug, gained an intense firsthand education in building and running successful businesses. He saw his parents and grandparents evaluate opportunities and weigh an investment's financial and social returns. He also vowed that he would never become an entrepreneur because he understood all too well the sacrifices it required. Instead, Speight attended his father's alma mater and studied engineering, specializing in industrial technology and computer-aided design (CAD). His father and grandfather would grill him on school breaks to explain how his education could be applied to business, but Speight insisted he wasn't interested. Speight had grown up a race-car fan and wanted to design Formula One cars for a living. But that's not the path he ended up following. After seven startups, his wife likes to remind him of his vow to resist the family's entrepreneurial instincts to no avail.

His life as an entrepreneur snuck up on him. After his junior year, he did an internship with Procter and Gamble, where he was given responsibility for managing the multinational company's archival engineering data and drawings. He scanned old print drawings and converted them to digital format. Back in school that fall, he compared notes with a classmate who'd done a similar internship with Philip Morris, and the two realized there was an opportunity to develop systems for managing those assets for large companies.

In 1995, the two classmates, both only 23 years old, started a company called C.O.R.E. Services that specialized in CAD, system design, and support for manufacturing, packaging, architectural, and civil engineering markets. Their first two customers would be Procter and Gamble and Philip Morris. Immediately acquiring two major corporate clients helped validate their idea and accelerated their traction with other businesses. Reflecting on that lucky break, Speight realized this was also a lucky break, the kind of opportunity many Black startup founders lack early on. He believed he was fortunate to start right out of the gate with that kind of affirmation from his industry. According to Speight, for Black entrepreneurs to thrive at scale, they need to find a way to incorporate some level of social proof that helps investors, customers, and other stakeholders overcome their initial perceived risk—with emphasis on "perceived"—of working with Black founders.

Soon, the co-founders expanded their offices to Colorado, Texas, and New Jersey. Because of customers like Miller Brewing Company and Budweiser in Colorado, they developed a specialty in bottling for the beverage industry. Going deep on a single vertical rather than across multiple sectors was a good move for the young company, and they were able to sell the business seven years later to a larger industrial design firm.

From his first foray as an entrepreneur, Speight gained some insights on the value he'd left on the table. Specifically, C.O.R.E. had passed on opportunities to patent new technology that could have been lucrative in their industry. After selling the company, Speight became intrigued by the commercialization of intellectual property. At the time, he happened to be serving on an advisory board at his alma mater, which had a few patents they didn't know what to do with. One, in particular, concerned manufacturing processes for nutraceuticals, or health supplements. With his experience at Procter and Gamble, Speight knew some people in the sector, so he flew to California, a nutraceuticals manufacturing hub, and managed to sell a license to the NC A&T technology right away. He returned to the college with a check for $100,000 and a deal for 3 percent of the gross profits on all materials made through that licensed process. The university, thrilled by the unexpected gains, asked him to start an office of intellectual property management.

To get a handle on how to support tech transfer commercialization, Speight contacted Mark Crowell, who he considers the "godfather of tech transfer," and who advised UNC-Chapel Hill and Duke. Crowell took the call cold and ended up talking with Doug for a couple of hours, walking him through every aspect he would need to consider. That generosity was another lesson. In spurring economic growth, it helps to have collaborators who are willing to invest in new people, rather than capturing more economic value for themselves. This develops the sector and community overall.

In his new role as director of the Office of Tech Transfer and his subsequent role as assistant vice chancellor for Outreach and Economic Development, Speight coached students and faculty on how to monetize their intellectual property, guiding them through licensing tech to industrial partners. Having developed a passion for the entrepreneurial life, he also encouraged innovators to establish their own startup companies when that path looked like a solid option.

Speight's tech transfer work soon caught the eye of NASA, which wanted to bring its portfolio of IP to market, both for commercialization purposes and to spur local economic development. He helped NASA establish partnerships with business incubators and universities, and managed tech transfer for three NASA field centers. Over the next few years, Speight continued to find ways to foster innovation through tech transfer, IP commercialization, joint venture partnerships, and startups. He became executive director of an angel investor fund specializing in tech. He worked with the Department of Energy and then with one of its sponsored science and technology laboratories, Oak Ridge National Laboratory, which was a partnership between the University of Tennessee and the Battelle Memorial Institute. He launched another company, Cathedral Innovation Group, to take advantage of opportunities he saw in financing equipment leasing for industrial 3-D printing.

Soon, Speight decided to move Cathedral from Tennessee to one of the country's more prominent fintech hubs. He chose Charlotte, North Carolina, to be closer to his extended family. However, Speight found the corporate culture in Charlotte lacking in entrepreneurial energy, so he decided to move again to an area more conducive to innovation and growth. This time he chose Durham, just as his grandfather had done 80 years prior.

Speight knew Durham is a very diverse city that has long supported economic opportunity for its Black citizenry. Created during the Black Wall Street days, Durham was home to companies like North Carolina Mutual Insurance, which was created at a time when Black people couldn't buy life insurance. North Carolina Mutual started with a simple goal of providing them with the dignity of being able to bury their dead. As it grew, it helped foster a professional class of Black people in Durham—lawyers, doctors, business owners—who continued to reinvest in their community across economic layers, some of whom even invested in Speight family businesses. While Durham's Black Wall Street was stifled after World War II, Speight and other entrepreneurs are now witnessing its revival. Over the past few years, there has been a push for more investment in Black founders in Durham, and it's starting to take off.

Speight's sister, Joye Speight, who had remained in Durham as an entrepreneur, reintroduced him to the community. Her startup had been supported by American Underground, a Google-sponsored startup hub for tech innovators. Speight became the organization's entrepreneur-in-residence, a yearlong fellowship designed to enable him to help fellow entrepreneurs at the hub. He was also asked to lead the local branch of a San Francisco–based program called CODE2040, a coding bootcamp designed to give Black and Latino entrepreneurs support in taking their own companies to the next level. After that, Speight was recruited to lead American Underground as its executive director, which he took on as part of his long-standing commitment to help other entrepreneurs and the startup community in general.

Speight considers himself a serial starter, not necessarily a serial entrepreneur. He thrives on identifying new market opportunities and building companies. He also feels a strong commitment to helping other entrepreneurs, especially in the minority startup community. To that end, he created AnnexTech Partners, which takes the divested software assets of major companies like Cisco Systems and develops new businesses around those technologies led by teams of minorities and women. He believes that tech has made a lot of broken promises to minorities but still has vast unrealized potential to improve lives through economic impact.

Speight has gone to countless venture capital conferences where there are always representatives from blue-chip funds talking about the dearth of investment in women and people of color, while acknowledging the industry's failure to allocate capital fairly. Time and again, the same investor says something along the lines of "I invested in these young kids who dropped out of college. I'm not sure this is even the right play for us. But they're smart and they'll figure it out." The kids in this scenario are almost always White. It never occurs to the investors that they're contradicting themselves. Speight accepts that this is how the industry works.

Fund managers, according to Speight, invest 80 percent of venture capital in White males and lose 99 percent of it on failed ventures. They make their money back on 1 percent of their bets. He believes that fund managers rarely examine the premise of their investments and expand their thesis. He wants to see a methodology developed for supporting Black entrepreneurs and Black startups. The capital is important, but more so are the intangibles like human behavior and mindsets. Like all founders, Black founders need access to opportunity with a low-risk threshold to learn how to build businesses that will succeed and grow.

For an industry that prides itself on being open to risk, investors can be very conservative and reluctant to enter into relationships with people they don't know. Speight has noticed that when venture investors in the Raleigh-Durham-Chapel Hill triangle are introduced to Black entrepreneurs, they'll question their experience or bona fides because they assume they would be a risky bet. They do not question why they may have heard of the White entrepreneurs already or know people who could vouch for them. This unconscious mindset perpetuates the cycle. Black entrepreneurs and their ideas go undersupported, just as Black markets, talent, and communities are overlooked. Everyone loses, including the investors.

Speight knows there's a need for investment in Black entrepreneurs that includes financial capital but encompasses much more. Like other successful Black entrepreneurs, he is driven to build that infrastructure of support so that the positive economic impact of innovation can be brought to scale.

Scaling the Impact of Innovation and Wealth Creation

Tennis superstar Serena Williams recognizes the need to fund minority startup founders who would otherwise lack access to capital, whose ventures serve overlooked market needs. She now leverages part of her wealth to this effect.

Williams is well-acquainted with the experience of being on the outside looking in. She emerged onto the professional tennis tour as a force of nature, playing a physically dominant style her competitors had never seen before. That she was Black and had grown up in relatively modest circumstances also upset the status quo. Tennis had long been a sport for wealthy Whites. Even the aesthetic of the game reinforced its country club exclusivity. White clothes. Pristine courts. Muted expressions of exuberance from players and audience members. Strictly enforced rules of personal conduct. Williams's skill and confidence enabled her to break down the explicit and implicit barriers to her Blackness, however psychologically challenging they might have been. Her closest analogue is Tiger Woods, another outsider who came to dominate a country club sport, and through that success gained enormous cultural and financial capital. When Williams retired from tennis in 2022, she was the highest-earning woman athlete of all time.

In 2014, closer to the end of her playing career than its beginning, Williams co-founded Serena Ventures, a venture capital (VC) firm to support startup founders "whose perspectives and innovations level the playing field for women and people of color." The fund quickly raised over $100 million in investment capital for early-stage startups in technology sectors. Soon, her ideas around investments and personal life would become even more closely aligned.

She married Reddit co-founder Alexis Ohanian in 2016. The next year, she became pregnant. During her prolonged labor, the baby's heart rate became erratic and the doctors decided to perform a C-section. When Williams woke, she immediately worried about the possibility of a blood clot. She'd suffered a pulmonary embolism in 2010 and knew she was at risk of another one after surgery, so she asked the nurses whether she should be on a heparin drip to thin her blood. The nurses dismissed her concerns because Serena was not a medical expert and heparin could exacerbate internal bleeding. But, falling in and out of consciousness and waking up to fits of coughing, excruciating pain in her lungs, and so much difficulty breathing that she needed an oxygen mask, Williams feared that she was dying. She kept fighting to be heard. She specifically asked for a bilateral CAT scan of her lungs, but her nurse answered, "I think all this medicine is making you talk crazy." She was told she needed rest.

Because of her coughing, however, her incisions burst, and Williams was brought back into surgery. Only then did her doctors do a scan and discover clots throughout her body. She spent the next six weeks bedridden, in danger for much of that time, and also suffering from post-partum depression but unbelievably lucky to have survived.

The news that Serena Williams nearly died from delivering her child was shocking to many who assumed that a wealthy woman in terrific physical health with access to the best care in the world would be fine. Others were not so shocked. Pregnancy, labor, and delivery are more dangerous than many realize, but they are especially dangerous for minorities. Black women are 2.4 to 3.3 times more likely to die of pregnancy-related causes than white women.[7] And Black women who are wealthy and have access to the best medical care like Serena Williams are still more likely to die than poor white women. Complex factors contribute to that awful reality, but the underlying reason is that Black women are not seen, heard, or valued in the same way as White women during their medical care.

Two years later, Williams's VC firm invested in Mahmee, a maternal and infant health tech company with a significant focus on ending the maternal mortality crisis for Black women. The startup was founded by Melissa Hanna, a Black woman whose mother was a pioneer in maternity and lactation programs.

Today, Williams's VC firm focuses on startups in health, wellness, and athletics. Her portfolio of companies includes Esusu, which helps people build credit through their rental payments (something that doesn't normally contribute to a credit score and creates another barrier for low-income borrowers); Noom, a health tech that tracks food intake and exercise to build healthier habits through empathetic support and coaching; Impossible Foods, a plant-based meat company; Tonal, a home smart gym; Teal Health, a women's health tech company focused on cervical cancer; Juno Medical, a virtual and in-office medical clinic; Sendwave, a US- and Senegal-based mobile money transfer company; Daily Harvest, a nutritious meal and food delivery company; and HUED, a company that measures, tracks, and trains healthcare organizations on health equity and culturally affirming care.

Of her portfolio of over 60 companies, 53 percent are started by women, 47 percent have Black founders, and 12 percent have Latino founders. When Serena Williams started her fund, less than 2 percent of investment capital went to women-founded companies, and minorities still represent a very small slice of most VC investment portfolios. Like competitive tennis, few clubs have been more exclusive than venture capital, and that problem persists. The barriers to access are complex and multifaceted. As with maternal death rates among Black women, even subtle biases and exclusions have an outsized impact. As Williams herself wrote, "Sometimes like attracts like. Men are writing those big checks to one another, and in order for us to change that, more people who look like me need to be in that position, giving money back to themselves."

Some will criticize the investment strategy as a variation of ESG (environmental, social, and governance), the investment approach that's highly criticized for applying non-financial factors to its investment criteria, despite many firms having a record of generating outsized returns. Williams says that she does not pick her founders based on their gender or the color of their skin; instead, she seeks investment opportunities that meet unmet or overlooked market needs. It so happens that female and non-White founders see market needs that others overlook because of their own lived experiences.

The Value of the Hidden Investor

One of the core themes of this book is that we all benefit when more of us succeed, and we all pay a price when more of us are prevented from succeeding. A powerful analogy for that conundrum comes from *The Sum of Us: What Racism Costs Everyone and How We Can Prosper Together* by Heather McGhee. The cover has a picture of a child jumping into a pool. In the 1920s through the 1940s, public funds helped build thousands of massive public pools around the United States. The goal was to give people who were not wealthy access to some of the pleasures and luxuries of the American Dream. While these pools were used by immigrants, they were off-limits, formally or informally, to Blacks until the 1960s, when civil rights legislation outlawed segregation. Black communities began to demand more benefits from their tax dollars. In response, White communities around the country began to close and even fill in their public pools—the very definition of a scenario in which everyone becomes worse off.

A century after Tulsa, and the destruction of other Black Wall Streets in cities across the South and Southwest, it's impossible to calculate how much wealth and prosperity was lost to us all when the industriousness, innovation, and entrepreneurial efforts of Black people were brutally oppressed. It's also impossible to know how much has been lost by preventing Black people from accessing the mortgages or loans they could have used to build their wealth, secure futures for their families, and send their children and grandchildren to better schools. All these and countless other injustices have harmed Blacks most obviously and directly, but harmed all Americans, including Whites.

A 2020 study by the Brookings Institute stated that "underrepresentation of Black businesses is costing the US economy millions of jobs and billions of dollars in unrealized revenues."[8] And the problem is not America's alone. A 2019 study by Boston Consulting Group estimates global GDP would be increased by $5 trillion annually if the number of women entrepreneurs equaled the number of men.[9]

At the same time, it's amazing to reflect on the accomplishments of Black American entrepreneurs, innovators, and wealth builders after the Civil War. In just a few generations, many Black people emerged from slavery to achieve wealth and prosperity on the dint of their entrepreneurial energy, their keen understanding of business, and the innovations they brought to market. It is easy to imagine the barriers they faced—the racism inflicted on them by individuals and systemic forces, their lack of resources and opportunities, and life-threatening dangers. But it is also worth examining the hidden history of their success and the forces and conditions that made it possible. In America, entrepreneurialism is highly prized but steeped in myth that holds that heroic individuals of rare ability succeed because they take great risks to make great things happen. While there is truth to that myth, it does not paint the whole picture or provide a practical and replicable formula.

Talent and determination only go so far. Entrepreneurial opportunity is facilitated, enhanced, and sometimes propelled by an interplay of factors. As Madam C. J. Walker's story illustrates, entrepreneurs and innovative ventures rarely come from nowhere to pioneer a new product, service, or idea. The drive or urge to build a business or bring an invention into the world can be idiosyncratic and complex. Not all entrepreneurs are well-balanced, emotionally grounded people with healthy upbringings! But as individuals, entrepreneurs are helped by having a certain level of education, know-how, and financial ability or support. They get inspiration from the circumstances around them and can be greatly influenced by role models. Without those influences, it can be difficult for anyone to imagine new possibilities or alternative paths. Even the ability to take risks and to make bold or courageous decisions—often thought of as individual or heroic acts—can be fostered and facilitated by emotional, financial, and social support.

The right economic and market conditions are also important. Those role models often seed the ground for future innovation through their success. The markets they develop create opportunities for competitors or new ideas and give backers more confidence to take risks with their capital. The wealth generated by those backers or employees bolsters the social infrastructure in a positive feedback loop. This is how economic growth creates prosperity, opportunity, and clusters of innovation.

In short, it takes individual, market, and community forces to make innovation and entrepreneurialism thrive and to grow personal wealth, organizational success, and community prosperity. Regardless of race, innovation and entrepreneurialism are challenging. But marginalized groups face particular challenges and barriers, and often seem to overcome those impediments through solutions that rely more on communal infrastructure and support. They also tend to meet market and societal needs that can be completely overlooked by the dominant social group. This appears to be true across all the marginalized groups we've studied, from European immigrant populations in the 1900s to Asian and Latino immigrant populations today. For Black Americans who were once enslaved, and overtly and systematically oppressed over the centuries since emancipation, the challenges and barriers to entrepreneurialism and wealth have been particularly formidable.

This makes the stories of Black American entrepreneurialism all the more important to highlight—though the history of Black entrepreneurialism, innovation, and wealth growth in America is filled with tragedy, injustice, and persistent barriers. This book focuses predominantly on success over failure, on possibility over unrealized hopes, on power gained over helplessness reinforced, and on the impact of entrepreneurial, business, and local community activities over political remedies. The deep-seated challenges and grim histories or facts are recognized and not shied away from, but the primary interest lies in how entrepreneurs and innovators have managed to overcome them and the impact they've made as a result.

The future is shaped by the stories we tell about the past and the present. The history of Black entrepreneurialism in America is rich, but much of that history is hidden. Even the story of the many Black Wall Streets—from Tulsa to Richmond and Durham and Atlanta—has been largely unknown until relatively recently. As they rise again and help modern Black venture investors and entrepreneurs, people like Doug Speight and Serena Williams create lasting economic impact for others. It becomes ever more important to examine the ingredients of success and how the formula can be brought to scale.

IT TAKES AN ENCLAVE

At Eshelman Innovation, the team continually strives to assess existing strengths or hidden natural advantages within the university setting and the surrounding region. Starting from strengths ensures that the innovation which emerges is cutting edge, as it is born from expertise or unique circumstances that allow it to scale in a competitive market. This is exactly why co-author John Bamforth found himself on his first trip to Rocky Mount, North Carolina, to visit his friend, Reuben Blackwell. This marked his initial venture into the Land of Tobacco and its long and somewhat challenging history. It was evident that the industry was far past its heyday, leaving behind a significant economic challenge. Despite this situation, John encountered a community driven to tackle this challenge and a leader in Reuben, who refused to let Rocky Mount be forgotten. Thus began a somewhat unusual but blessed friendship between a child of the civil rights movement and a working-class chap from an old coal-mining town in the north of England.

The Tar River starts at the foothills of the Uwharrie Mountains, the oldest mountain range in North America. From there, it travels southeast on a meandering 200-mile journey through present-day North Carolina to the Pamlico Sound, the largest lagoon along the East Coast. Where the Piedmont Plateau ends and the Atlantic Coastal Plain begins, the river drops; it's more like a giant step down than a true waterfall. The rolling hills suddenly flatten. For European colonists traveling upstream, this elevation change marked the end of easy navigation but the possibility of future industry. The village of Rocky Mount was established a mile from those falls, taking its name from a nearby rocky outcrop, and gaining its economic status from the dam that was built to generate power for sawmills and cotton mills.

Today, Rocky Mount is a small but dynamic city in the new South, with a population that is 64 percent Black, 26 percent White, and 0.5 percent Native American. In many ways, it exists as both a monument to a troubled past and a living symbol of a still challenging but highly promising future. It also illustrates the promise of modern enclaves and how the civil rights initiatives going back a century continue to foster social support today, tapping the resilience of local communities mired in a history of slavery, institutional racism, and economic oppression, while nurturing the conditions necessary for economic progress.

The Black Belt and Great Migration

Centuries before Rocky Mount became a mill town or a stop on the Tar River, the Tuscarora people, a Native American tribe originally from the

Great Lakes region, had migrated to eastern Carolina and settled there, becoming the most populous tribe in the region. By the mid-1600s, the Tuscarora had developed an active and peaceful trading relationship with the European colonists. The goods, firearms, and resources they traded for helped the Tuscarora prosper and dominate other tribes in the area. Tensions grew, however, as the American settlers expanded westward, seizing land for farming and kidnapping Tuscarora people to work those fields as slaves. A bloody and protracted war broke out in 1711, which resulted in the Tuscarora's defeat a few years later. Many of the survivors returned north as refugees, joining the mighty Iroquois Confederacy.

The rich farmland was perfect for growing tobacco and cotton. With fewer enslaved Tuscarora people available to them, the settlers turned increasingly to Africa for new sources of labor to meet the worldwide demand for textiles and tobacco. South Carolina even began to regulate and organize its overseas slave trade to accommodate the growing need. In 1767, there were 41,000 African Americans enslaved in North Carolina. By 1860, there were over 330,000.

The richness of the soil was remarkable. North and South Carolina are near the tail end of a fertile strip of land that stretches across 623 counties along the South and up the East Coast from East Texas to Virginia. This agricultural crescent has become known as the Black Belt, as much for the darkness of the rich, black soil as for the dark skin of the enslaved people who were forced to work the cotton and tobacco fields. That labor was brutal, back-breaking work. Each cotton tuft was plucked by hand and crammed into sacks, which quickly grew too heavy and cumbersome to haul. The only reprieve was Sunday, held aside for worship, communal gatherings, singing, and even dressing up.

Despite lacking any agency over their labor or persons, the culture, community, and spirituality of enslaved African Americans took root and flourished in that soil, not unlike the crops they harvested. Their numbers also grew. At the time of the first US census in 1790, 760,000 African Americans lived in the young nation, the vast majority in the Black Belt territories. By the start of the Civil War, there were 4.4 million. According to the census of 1910, 90 percent of African Americans in the United States still lived in the Black Belt, almost half a century after emancipation, despite Jim Crow laws that institutionalized racist policies. Some, able to earn a living wage, began to build an independent economic life for themselves and even prosper. By 1920, just as Black Wall Streets had arisen in cities throughout the South and up the East Coast, Black-owned farms spread throughout the Black Belt. In a country of 100 million people, a million African Americans owned farms. Though small and family-operated, those farms collectively amounted to 41.4 million acres of land.

That was the peak of Black farmland ownership. The number of acres and farmers declined rapidly over the next few decades. Much as the merchants, shop owners, innkeepers, and bankers of Black Wall Streets saw their efforts and ambitions thwarted by violent, political, and legal forces, so the Black farmers suffered because of complex legal, societal, and economic factors that were often deliberately designed to reverse their progress and end their prosperity. Some of their land was seized through violent or dubiously legal means. Some farmers found land ownership increasingly impossible because of racist policies and practices, including a systematic lack of access to government and bank-sponsored loans, discriminatory railroad rates, usurious prices for farm machinery and fertilizer, targeted tariffs and taxes, local corruption, and government support for large, industrial farms at the expense of smaller family farms.

Those combined forces took their toll. Today, there are around 40,000 black farmers in America. Collectively, they own less than 1 percent of American farmland or around 4.7 million acres (compared to 41.4 million in 1920).[1] Though family farming is a difficult, precarious life for Whites as well as Blacks, the 94 percent decline in Black farm ownership over the past hundred years is striking, as it represents three times the decline of White farm ownership.[2]

Starting in 1910, an enormous change took place in the distribution of the American population. In a period known as the first Great Migration, around 2 million Black Americans left the South for the industrial cities of the Northeast and Midwest, including New York, Chicago, Detroit, Pittsburgh, and Indianapolis. They left because of the legal and cultural racism of the South and the violence and oppression it engendered. The gains of Reconstruction had been largely pulled back by the Redemption movement and the rise of the KKK. The Black Americans who moved north were drawn by good-paying jobs and the chance for greater personal freedom. World War I had sent men to Europe to fight and stifled the steady flow of immigrants from Europe. Suddenly the factories of the Midwest and Northeast were in dire need of labor, and Black Americans seized the opportunity to leave their small farms and the subsistence-level existence of sharecropping.

The safety and belonging they sought were not as easy to find. Racial violence surged around the country after World War I, even in the cities of the North, and especially Chicago, where hostility toward Blacks had grown with the sudden shift in demographics. For Black soldiers who'd fought for their country in Europe and returned to America, this was an especially bitter turn.

The Great Migration slowed during the Great Depression, when jobs became scarce, but it surged again following World War II. By 1970, another 4 million Black Americans had left the South. This time their migration extended to the Southwest and West, including Los Angeles, San Francisco, Oakland, Portland, and Seattle. Once again, institutional barriers arose. Black people experienced housing discrimination, redlining, and restrictive covenants that segregated cities into White and Black neighborhoods and perpetuated racial disparities and inequities in health, environment, housing, income, and education that persist to this day.

In 1900, 89 percent of Black Americans lived in the South. By 1970, that percentage had fallen to 53 percent.[3] The South suffered as a result of a weakened agriculture sector, the loss of skilled labor, and a loss of cultural and social dynamism. The South's loss was the rest of the country's gain. Despite effective segregation of neighborhoods in the North and West, new enclaves formed, and Black culture flourished with distinct music, food, and literature.

The story of Rocky Mount might seem like a small one amid a century of national turmoil and change, but its history and present circumstances illustrate the struggle and potential of a changing world.

Rocky Mount's Rise and Fall and Rise Again

The river, the falls, the geographic location, and the richness of the Black Belt soil gave Rocky Mount many advantages. The navigable waters had always drawn settlers—first Native Americans, then European colonists. The falls generated power after a dam was constructed in the early 1800s. A cotton gin was built in 1811 and a sawmill in 1830. A 20-acre complex rose to house workers and store produce in warehouses. The climate and the rich soil of the Black Belt helped cotton and tobacco plants thrive. The town's location, 58 miles east of Raleigh, 60 miles south of Virginia, and 144 miles north of Wilmington, gave it proximity to three economic power regions. A railroad transported goods and people to Virginia in the north and the port of Wilmington in the south, and from there to the Atlantic Ocean and the world.

Enslaved people and underpaid Black workers were critical to the early prosperity of Rocky Mount. The enslaved worked the cotton mills, fields, and railroad loading docks until emancipation. Cotton became less profitable when global prices fell, so Rocky Mount, like most of North Carolina, turned more of its fields over to tobacco. The mass production of cigarettes opened new markets around the world and gave rise to major companies like Duke, Reynolds, Liggett, and the American Tobacco Company. With emancipation and specialization, jobs quickly became segregated by race. White women and children replaced the slaves at the cotton mill. Blacks continued to do hard labor in the fields but received less pay than Whites for the same work. Black tobacco workers organized a strike to secure higher wages, but the strike failed and the workers returned to their old jobs at their old pay.

By then, Rocky Mount was home to about 3,000 people. Within a few years, the population doubled and the city incorporated, spurred by strong economic growth. It even established an active central business district. At first, the city was sharply segregated by race; then those boundaries were changed to keep Whites in an advantageous position. The central rail line neatly divides the city between two counties, Edgecombe and Nash, which reflect very different racial realities to this day—one majority Black, the other majority White. Early on, Black political power grew in Edgecombe County, which was home to one of the largest populations of formerly enslaved people in the state. The residents began to elect their Black officials and exert power and influence in state politics. So, in 1871, the North Carolina General Assembly moved the county border to dilute the voting power of Black people and shift the more economically prosperous areas of the city into the predominantly White county. Blacks were not allowed to work or even shop at White businesses.

Once again, the Black community adapted. A Black business district known as Douglas Block rose to meet the needs of the community. It contained a pharmacy, a hotel, barbershops and salons, dentists, doctors, restaurants, and even funeral homes.

The city was segregated culturally, too. Every year, at the end of the tobacco season, White townspeople hosted a debutante ball in one of the giant tobacco warehouses. These events, known as June Germans, started in 1870. The national press covered it like the Kentucky Derby. Jazz and blues bands from around the country came to perform and brought with them many of the greatest musicians in history, like Louis Armstrong, Count Basie, Sarah Vaughan, Ella Fitzgerald, and John Coltrane, who made Rocky Mount a must-stop on their national tours.

Those musicians couldn't stay at White hotels. Instead, they turned to the Green Book, which helped them safely navigate the roads and hotels of the segregated South. The Green Book led them to Rocky Mount's Black hotel instead. Black middle-class families, living in large and beautiful homes close to downtown, also rented rooms to guests and visitors when the hotel was booked. Black audiences couldn't join Whites at dance parties, so they started their own Colored June German on the Monday after the White June German weekend. Those world-famous Black performers would stick around for the Monday event and let loose in an all-night dance party that featured one band after the other. By the 1930s, the Colored June German regularly out-drew the Whites-only version, and thousands of black people from around the state would converge on Rocky Mount to join the fun.

Despite the energy and dynamism of Black culture in Rocky Mount, economic progress and prosperity were not equitably shared by the powers that be. Infrastructure investment—paved streets, lights, sewer lines—went to White neighborhoods while Black communities were neglected. Economic programs designed to support and train workers, increase employment, and lift citizens out of poverty were manipulated by local administrators to omit Black participants.[4] Over different decades, striking workers led grassroots efforts for better pay, but discrimination remained a powerful countervailing force.

Perhaps it was this spirit of resilience that inspired Dr. Martin Luther King, Jr., when he visited Rocky Mount in 1962. In his speech at Booker T. Washington High School before 1,800 people, King used the famous phrase "I have a dream" for the first time, a year before the remarkable oration he gave at the end of the legendary March on Washington. As King said near the end of his speech:

> *I have a dream that one day right here in Rocky Mount, the sons of former slaves and the sons of former slave owners will meet at the table of brotherhood, knowing that one God brought man to the face of the Earth. I have a dream tonight that one day my little daughter and my two sons will grow up in a world not conscious of the color of their skin, but only conscious of the fact that they are members of the human race. . . .[5]*

But how to make that happen? King believed that economic justice, security, and opportunity were essential to achieving true freedom and equality. He called for fair wages, quality education, the ability to unionize, and community self-reliance and empowerment. As he observed, "Jobs are more difficult to create than voting roles."[6]

To help create that kind of security and opportunity, others would need to step forward. They did.

A Dream in Action

Leon Sullivan was born in 1922 in Charleston, West Virginia. Raised in a poor neighborhood, his early experiences with racism and economic discrimination inspired him to fight for civil rights all his life. He was a physically and intellectually impressive man who, at six-foot-five, towered over most people. He seemed destined to be a preacher or an athlete, and for a time he was both. A minister at 18, he was also a talented basketball and football player who received an athletic scholarship to West Virginia State College. An injury ended his playing career almost before it started, but Sullivan managed to pay for school by working in a steel mill. The education at one of the nation's historically Black colleges and universities (HBCUs) and the experience of hard mill labor would guide his path and influence the lives of many others to this day.

West Virginia State College was established in 1891. The British originally gave the land to George Washington for his service in the French and Indian War; then Washington sold it to a plantation owner who quickly brought on slave labor. In 1853, Samuel Cabell, the son of the Virginia governor at the time, was next to buy the land. Cabell had been a slave owner himself until he married one of the enslaved women, and together they had 13 children. Through persistent and complicated legal means, Cabell officially emancipated his wife and children and ensured that they would inherit his wealth. He was murdered near the end of the Civil War by a group of White men who hated him for those efforts, though they were found innocent at trial. A decade later, Cabell's daughter sold some of the land to create the West Virginia Colored Institute to give her children and those of their community a place to go to school. That's the HBCU school where Leon Sullivan became steeped in history and education.

After graduating from West Virginia State College, Sullivan was unsure what he should do next. Then he heard the famous Reverend Adam Clayton Powell give a talk. Powell had grown up in small-town Virginia as a free person. Like Sullivan, he'd worked in steel mills to make his way while attending college at Wayland Seminary, an HBCU in Washington, DC. After graduating, Powell studied at Yale Divinity School and then embarked on a series of ministries throughout the Northeast before landing at Abyssinian Baptist Church in Harlem, New York. Powell convinced Sullivan that he should do the same thing. Harlem was one of the new epicenters of African American culture in the Northeast, a destination for many Blacks in the first Great Migration. Sullivan followed their path and continued his divinity studies at graduate school while also serving as Powell's assistant at Abyssinian.

A few years later, Sullivan got his own congregation, first in New Jersey and then in Philadelphia. In each position, he took an active and outspoken role in the growing civil rights movement. He believed that work, wealth generation, and ownership were critical for improving the lives and social standing of Black people. As part of his activism, he began lobbying large corporations to establish inclusive hiring practices. When those companies did not respond to his demands, he convened hundreds of other pastors to organize boycotts in their communities and apply pressure on those companies. Their efforts were remarkably successful. The targeted companies agreed to hire more Black people, and that progress brought Sullivan to Dr. Martin Luther King, Jr.'s attention. Together they created Operation Breadbasket, an organization for improving Black communities.

Sullivan knew that many Black people needed training, education, and even basic life skills to get good jobs, budget their money, attain suitable housing, and lift themselves out of poverty. To that end, he founded another community-based organization called Opportunities Industrialization Centers of America (OIC), which offered training programs and job-seeking assistance. As Sullivan suspected, the need for such programs was almost limitless, and soon 60 affiliated centers spread to 30 states.

In 1969, an OIC location was established in the town of Rocky Mount, North Carolina. That's where Reuben Blackwell entered the picture. Raised in a movement household by parents who were educators and activists, Blackwell was a child of the civil rights era. He went to school at UNC-Chapel Hill and was recruited to lead Reverend Sullivan's Rocky Mount OIC in 1998.

Following the plan laid out by Reverend Sullivan, the Rocky Mount OIC served as an education-based organization. The focus was on job training and life-skills development. Founded by Rocky Mount Black business and political leaders, OIC in Rocky Mount became a force that advocated for social integration and economic improvement through job preparation skills for Black people who wanted to enter the industrial workforce. From 1969 to 1998, the Rocky Mount OIC had built a solid reputation for creating pathways of success for thousands of poor and working-class Black families as they yearned for economic independence. OIC also had become an agency that partnered with the North Carolina Department of Health and Human Services to provide outreach programs to combat the growing spread of HIV in Black communities in eastern North Carolina. After he was recruited to lead and expand the OIC programs and footprint, Blackwell quickly realized that the community's challenges went even deeper than Sullivan's mandate. One of those challenges was the need to shift mindsets cultivated by the persistent history of the community, one steeped in racism and hopelessness.

Blackwell grew up in a little town north of Durham, and he had never seen cotton fields until he came to Rocky Mount. But as soon as he did, he could imagine the hard labor in the endless fields of cotton. He soon understood how hard it is for people to go from the cotton fields to falling in love with the idea of having a job. Someone else still owns your labor. Under Blackwell's leadership, the OIC Rocky Mount started rethinking its role and the support it could provide. Blackwell spent a lot of time helping people appreciate that their own dreams were valid and legitimate and that they could pursue them by setting specific intentions and building a path to success. That work went beyond training and included coaching people to develop their own networks, teaching them how to manage their finances and develop more personal security, and even how to build their own businesses and succeed in competitive markets so they can gain more of the benefits of their hard work.

One of the OIC's programs, the Integrated Training Academy, initially invested in by the Golden LEAF Foundation, is a workforce development initiative that creates credentialed career pathways for people to develop enhanced skills across many professions, from healthcare to construction, manufacturing, and logistics. Another program, the Black Entrepreneurial Network, serves as a hub for Black innovators and startup founders. Both programs are housed in a tobacco warehouse where slaves once worked, and where Black workers formed the first union in North Carolina in 1946. Today, the children and grandchildren of those people are working to build their own businesses. A lasting legacy, as Blackwell notes, is created not by giving your job to your children but by passing it on to them.

The OIC's work has also expanded beyond individuals to serve the community. Like Reverend Sullivan, Blackwell's approach to meeting the needs of his constituents can best be described as social entrepreneurship. It involves galvanizing an array of forces—political leaders, grassroots activists, community-based organizations, local businesses, philanthropists, local institutions (educational, religious), and everyday people—to create and operate programs that solve local social or economic issues. Health, for example, was a major issue. As a crossroads town, the sex industry in Rocky Mount had always been active, and HIV infection rates were higher than the national average. The OIC was enlisted to join other organizations in helping with community outreach to provide testing and education on healthy sex behaviors. They quickly made a lot of headway, but Blackwell was bothered by how the pervasive lack of access to healthcare in the community created a barrier to economic and social progress. He'd recently met a group of young women participating in the OIC job-training program who couldn't interview for the jobs they'd trained for because they were unable to obtain pre-qualifying medical exams. The reason? A lack of available healthcare providers.

Many of the Medicaid-funded primary care practices had closed down for a variety of frustrating reasons, including the financial challenges inherent in providing services through Medicaid programs. That left few affordable care options for the community. For those six Black women, the only clinic in town that accepted Medicaid had a strict policy on missed appointments. If you missed three appointments, you couldn't get another one. Each of the women had exceeded their allotment of missed appointments because of challenges related to childcare, elder care, transportation, and other issues of daily life. Now they couldn't get the jobs that would help solve some of their economic and personal problems.

At a meeting in Greenville to celebrate the OIC's success with its HIV program, Blackwell had a cloud hanging over his head. Speaker after speaker praised their work, but all he could think about was the people in the community who faced other health challenges beyond HIV. His father, for instance, suffered from diabetes but didn't have the medical or social support to overcome his eating habits or nutrition challenges. For each person like that in Blackwell's life, he knew there were thousands more. Suddenly, in the middle of the celebration, Blackwell erupted, years of frustration pouring out. He contrasted the success they'd just achieved with the larger but quieter healthcare problems that even more people faced, ranging from access to care to other social barriers to health. "The state," he said, "has failed us."[7]

Across the table, an older White man looked over his glasses and spoke quietly. "Well, why don't you do something about it?"

The man was Jim Bernstein. Though Blackwell had never met him before and knew nothing about him, Bernstein was a significant figure in rural health. A graduate of Johns Hopkins, he'd immediately joined the Peace Corps, served two years in Morocco, then got his master's degree in hospital administration. With that background, he'd become the director of Indian Health Services in New Mexico until he moved to North Carolina to study his deep passion, rural health, at UNC. Upon graduating, he was chosen, while still in his twenties, to be the first director of the North Carolina Office of Rural Health. Under his leadership, 81 community-owned rural health centers had been established across the state, drawing nearly 2,000 primary care providers. At the time of the meeting with Blackwell, he was near the end of his long career but still president of the National Rural Health Association. In other words, Bernstein knew what he was talking about, though Blackwell didn't know that yet.

Instead, Blackwell felt his umbrage rise. He thought Bernstein was throwing the problem back in his face and protested that there were no easy solutions. Bernstein didn't take offense but persisted.

"Why don't you start a health clinic?" he asked.

Blackwell offered a list of reasons it couldn't be done, and Bernstein countered each one in turn.

Blackwell: "I don't know how to do it."
Bernstein: "I'll find you a mentor."
Blackwell: "We don't have the money."
Bernstein: "We'll find you the money."
Blackwell: "There are so many other resources we don't have."
Bernstein: "We'll connect you to people who can help."

Then, Bernstein added, "You can do this if you're willing. And you must be willing." And Blackwell, who knew it was one of the most important things he could do, said yes.

The two men never had another conversation. Bernstein died shortly after. But before then, Bernstein made connections for Blackwell with government officials, foundations, and a medical network. With that support, the Rocky Mount OIC went into the healthcare business and opened an FQHC (federally qualified health clinic) to provide primary care to the community. Sadly, Blackwell's father died three days before the ribbon-cutting ceremony at the new clinic. Blackwell missed his own father's wake because of how busy those first days were, but he knew that his father would rather he focus on his work to give others a better chance to live.

Blackwell's commitment to provide health services has only deepened since. For Blackwell, healthcare is central to our lives and our history. Today, Rocky Mount has three full-time primary care sites, as well as a dental practice, a behavioral health practice, an urgent care clinic, and two pharmacies. Yet challenges still exist for the Black citizens of Rocky Mount. Black people occupy the lowest rungs of every meaningful economic, social, or educational statistic, revealing the persistent disparity. The community is still racially divided. Despite there being twice as many Black people as Whites in Rocky Mount, it wasn't until the late 1990s that Black officials secured a majority on the city council. Too often, the progress the OIC makes is met by pervasive biases and criticism. However, the OIC continues to work to empower the children and grandchildren of the Black Belt with the resources and support they need to rise above.

That work is bearing fruit. Fifteen years ago, *Forbes* listed Rocky Mount as one of the poorest cities in America. In 2019, *Forbes* declared Rocky Mount one of the best small cities to do business.[8] Douglas Block, the early Black Wall Street, is being restored, and a Rocky Mount Event Center has been built on the Edgecombe side and attracts thousands of young families to downtown Rocky Mount every weekend. In 2021, the Robert Wood Johnson Foundation recognized Rocky Mount as a Culture of Health Prize winner for its success in advancing health, opportunity, and equity.

Robert Wood Johnson's vision centered around the organic growth and development of individuals and communities. Blackwell fully supported this approach and believed the OIC of Rocky Mount deserved the honor bestowed by the foundation. They had achieved great success by rallying the efforts of those striving for a better life and community. Improvements were focused on addressing the specific needs of the community. As Blackwell and the members of OIC demonstrate, true innovation doesn't originate from the top down, but rather rises up from the grassroots level.

It Takes an Enclave

A year after Dr. Martin Luther King, Jr., gave his "I Have a Dream" speech at the high school in Rocky Mount, he gave another version at the Second African Baptist Church in Savannah, Georgia. In that speech, King noted that a century earlier, in 1864, on the steps of Second Baptist, General William Tecumseh Sherman had read the Emancipation Proclamation, which declared that all men held as slaves henceforth would be free. Yet, he stated plainly, "One hundred years later, the Negro still is not free."

King was known for connecting with the local audiences when he spoke, drawing on aspects of their unique circumstances and history and tying those details to the universal struggle of Black people in particular, but also humanity as a whole. His "I Have a Dream" speech encapsulates the universality of his view. King was a humanist, an activist, a community leader, and an orator. Like a social entrepreneur, he was driven to address social inequities and help people rise above them.

The church he spoke at was one of the earliest Black churches in the nation and it was marked by a red door. The red door was an old Christian symbol indicating that sanctuary could be found within. But in the Black Christian tradition, the red door also signified that Black people owned the property. The church, in that sense, was a symbol of both sanctuary and ownership.

Throughout Black American history, the sense of community found behind those red doors had been a source of the social entrepreneurship that Dr. King, Reverend Sullivan, and Reverend Powell brought to communities all over the country. Likewise, it was where business entrepreneurs like Madam C. J. Walker had found their support networks to bring products and services to Black customers.

Black churches, Black community groups, Black colleges, Black Wall Streets, Black performers, and the Black Belt itself helped foster the enclaves that have created economic opportunities for generations of Black people and helped communities flourish. But despite its importance to Black churchgoers, the red door was never meant to be a barrier to others. Just as Dr. Martin Luther King, Jr., had called for a world in which one day the children of slaves and the children of slave owners would sit at the same banquet, the church was open to all. King was not an exclusionist. He believed that Black people needed their own community and sense of ownership, but he believed the strength of that community would help all prosper, not just Blacks.

King had seen this kind of community and prosperity growing up in Atlanta. In its early history, the city had been an enclave for Black people who created their own businesses, organizations, institutions, and cultural events. The business district known as Sweet Auburn Historic District became a kind of Black Wall Street to the Black community of Atlanta. Businesses, hotels, pharmacies, restaurants, grocery stores, and performance halls flourished there.

Segregation was real. But throughout the decades, Atlanta's prosperity increased as people flocked to the city from rural areas across the Black Belt. The civil rights movement catalyzed more prosperity and power. Black businesses thrived. Black political leaders were voted into key positions, including mayor.

Today, the city is considered by many the Black mecca of America, a place of economic opportunity where Blacks can enter the upper-middle and upper classes; where Black educational institutions continue to foster new generations; where Black culture is expressed and celebrated in art, music, television, and movies. In today's Black Belt, Blacks still outnumber Whites, and the region has the highest poverty rate in the nation, among the highest mortality and unemployment rates, and education levels that rank in the bottom third. But the area is also experiencing a resurgence and shows very real signs of becoming the locus of a new economic, political, and social prosperity.

Atlanta's story is part of the larger story of the greater South. According to census statistics, a new Great Migration is well underway, as college-educated young Black Americans from the North and West are returning in ever-growing numbers to the South and Southeast.[9] That migration started in the 1970s as northern cities like Detroit deindustrialized, costing many jobs. It picked up pace in the 1990s and continues to grow today, largely catalyzed by new investment in civic infrastructure, education, and economic opportunity. This time, urban centers are the destination, not the rich farmland of the Black Belt. But those migrants are drawn to the historically Black regions of the South and Southeast particularly because of the ties of culture, family, history, shared identity, and opportunities for professional networking. The sense of home, belonging, and safety have created the kind of enclave that the residents of Rocky Mount would understand. It's not about isolating from the rest of the world, but about sharing resources, support, and common experience to venture out, overcome all obstacles, and establish new footholds for success.

THE ENCLAVE OF EDUCATION

Despite the abolition of slavery in 1865, Blacks were forbidden from attending most colleges and universities of the South for the next hundred years. The Morrill Act of 1862 was passed to create land-grant colleges in the United States funded by the sale of federally owned land. (That land was often seized or coerced from Native American tribes.) The second iteration of the Morrill Act passed in 1890 legalized the separation of Whites and Blacks in education, but required all states to establish land-grant colleges for Blacks if segregation laws forbade them from attending the existing land-grant colleges. The national system of historic Black colleges and universities (HBCUs) arose to help meet this requirement. The majority of HBCUs were formed in the Black Belt region, where former slaves were numerous and Jim Crow segregation laws persisted until the passage of civil rights legislation in 1965. The Freedmen's Bureau helped fund them.

HBCUs have become centers for Black educational achievement and driving forces in the development of a Black middle class. Collectively, they have helped nurture generations of Black scientists, engineers, writers, thinkers, politicians, and business leaders. Today, there are 101 HBCUs in the US, producing nearly 20 percent of all Black college graduates. HBCUs are responsible for 25 percent of all Black STEM graduates. Most of the nation's Black judges, 40 percent of the Black members of Congress, and half the Black doctors in the nation graduated from HBCUs. Though only 3 percent of the total number of colleges and universities, they account for 13 percent of all Black graduates.[1]

Partly funded by state and federal grants today, HBCUs have always struggled with sustaining adequate financial resources. The top 10 predominantly White colleges and universities in the country had endowments totaling $200 billion in 2020, compared to $2 billion for the top 10 HBCUs. Like many institutions across the country, HBCUs have experienced budgetary pressure for academic programs, amenities, student housing, and aging buildings. HBCUs have also suffered from a perception that they are second-tier institutions compared to elite, predominantly White colleges, which offer more financial incentives and resources. In contrast, the majority of students attending HBCUs come from low-income households.[2]

Yet HBCUs are also recognized as safe, secure, mentally healthy environments for Black students to feel seen, heard, and empowered. Anecdotally, students prioritizing safer, more inclusive learning environments and parents prioritizing their children's mental health over their academic status seem to be contributing to a recent rise in enrollment. Howard University's enrollment numbers increased 28 percent between 2019 and 2021. Morgan State's enrollment jumped 8 percent. North Carolina A&T's rose

6 percent. All during a period that saw national enrollments drop 5 percent because of the pandemic.[3]

Perhaps the sentiment was expressed by Nikole Hannah-Jones. Jones, a professor, was offered a faculty chair position with tenure at the University of North Carolina at Chapel Hill, but the Board of Trustees denied her tenure, only to reverse its decision later due to legal threats and public outcry. Jones decided to stop fighting for the appointment at the UNC, and instead she chose Howard University.

> *I have decided that instead of fighting to prove I belong at an institution that until 1955 prohibited Black Americans from attending, I am instead going to work in the legacy of a university not built by the enslaved but for those who once were. For too long, Black Americans have been taught that success is defined by gaining entry to and succeeding in historically White institutions. I have done that, and now I am honored and grateful to join the long legacy of Black Americans who have defined success by working to build up their own.*[4]

But enclaves of education can be created more broadly, and programs can steer Black students toward entrepreneurship and wealth creation.

Today, at age 60, Bernard Bell is the executive director of the Shuford Program in Entrepreneurship at the University of North Carolina at Chapel Hill, his alma mater, where he helps nurture entrepreneurs and entrepreneurial ventures.[5] Before then, he was the program's entrepreneur-in-residence. Bell returned to UNC-Chapel Hill after a few decades of building innovative new television networks and dabbling in Silicon Valley technology companies. Throughout his life, he's benefitted from the power of enclaves to provide the kind of nurturance, support, guidance, and psychological safety that may not be essential for success in entrepreneurialism, but it sure doesn't hurt.

His first enclave was his grandfather's 273-acre tobacco farm outside Greensboro, North Carolina. It was his grandfather's second farm. He lost the first in a bad lend-lease deal to a White man who took advantage of his inability to read or write. As a result, the family was turned out of their house and kicked off their land when Bell's father was 13. Over a decade later, Bell's father helped Bell's grandfather buy a new farm with the soldier's pay he'd saved diligently while serving in World War II.

The new tobacco farm became the focus of the rapidly growing Bell family. Bell's grandparents had 13 children, 34 grandchildren, and, eventually, 56 great-grandchildren. Bell and his twin sister were the youngest grandchildren. The farm employed about 90 people, 30 of whom were family. This was Bell's grandfather's way of keeping the family connected. He was a believer in teaching life lessons about work ethic and the value of tending crops with patience, consistency, and care, and he was not above the occasional scare tactic. One of his grandfather's favorite admonitions was "If you don't work, you don't eat," and while it was meant metaphorically, Bell and the other grandchildren took him quite seriously and paid attention to whatever their grandfather told them to do.

Later, Bell realized that his grandfather was the first entrepreneur he ever knew. Even though farming was arduous, dirty work, the enterprise itself was actually a very complex business operation with a number of departments and many different job descriptions. It was Bell's job to distribute the paychecks every Friday, and he learned to appreciate the impact that work had on people's lives and well-being.

His second enclave was the community he grew up in. Despite his farm roots, Bell was raised in a very academic, almost suburban environment. His father was the first person in his family to go to college and returned from the Second World War to finish his degree and eventually earn his

PhD in agriculture science. Bell's mother grew up north of Raleigh-Durham in a beautiful colonial house. Her father was a photographer who invested in real estate and built the first school in their community for Black children. Though he died young in a tragic car accident, the family remained prosperous enough for all six daughters to go to college and eventually earn graduate degrees.

It took Bell a long time to appreciate how rare his upbringing was compared to many other Black Americans. His middle-class, all-Black community was a close-knit and comfortable place to live. His neighbors were dentists, doctors, teachers, and professors. Bell was able to walk to school and church. His classroom and Sunday school teachers were neighborhood people who knew his family and cared about his well-being. His father was chair of the department of agriculture at the historically Black college North Carolina A&T and president of the university senate. He had his own office with a large desk, a leather swivel chair, and a secretary stationed outside. At university ceremonies, he led processions carrying the senate scepter. Bell's mother had a degree in psychology and taught at the community college. The family home was large and modern, with rooms for everyone. They played music over the intercom and frequently had large groups of friends over for dinner parties and backyard cookouts. That atmosphere of acceptance, belonging, and security instilled a natural confidence in Bell, and a healthy sense of entitlement.

What he didn't perceive until later was how hard his parents and their friends worked to preserve that sense of comfort, security, empowerment, and pride in identity and origin. Though his father earned his PhD in 1964, he couldn't vote until the Voting Rights Act of 1965. When his parents bought their house in 1968, there were still laws on the books that prevented Black people from borrowing more than $13,000 for a house, which forced Bell's parents to delay their home purchase for years until they'd saved enough cash. Though his parents had a rich social life and got dressed up in fancy black ties and gowns for various neighborhood balls and events, they couldn't eat in restaurants.

The world outside looked bad on television, but that was in distinct contrast to the life he had experienced. He saw riots and attack dogs and firehoses on the news, but never heard the "n" word in real life. Instead of conflict and despair, his parents and their friends engaged in passionate, sophisticated conversations about politics, history, and civil rights. They shared stories about the history of Black people in America that informed Bell's understanding of the struggle since 1619, but Bell saw only the gains and the prosperity.

In fact, Bell didn't even know any White children until he was in his early teens. That's when busing, the policy of racial integration that brought Black children to White schools and vice versa, began. Even then, however, Bell's experience of racial integration turned out to be positive. Though his school was now 60 percent Black and 40 percent White, the students all got along. Bell wonders if the students did so well together because they shared similar values around family, education, and hard work. Most had come from educated families like his own with farming or blue-collar backgrounds in the not-so-distant past. They were all expected to study hard and meet expectations, so they did. The friendships he made then have endured to a remarkable extent. Bell's still part of a group of 65 students, Black and White, who went to school together and continue to meet monthly, decades later.

In retrospect, however, Bell realizes how much his parents and their friends had prepared their children to succeed in a White world. They were taught to dress up for special occasions, stay quiet and polite around adults, and always act on their best behavior. At school, they were supposed to work hard, stay out of trouble, do what they were told, and remain composed, no matter what happened. While this served him well in some aspects of his professional life, opening doors and giving him exposure to opportunities, the deference, reserve, and even timidity he was taught also hindered him. They may have helped a Black person survive and get along in a White-dominated world, but they were not the attitudes or behaviors of a successful executive or entrepreneur making their mark or carving their own path.

Bell learned this after graduating from college. At UNC-Chapel Hill, he studied economics and math, excelling as in high school. Because of the prestige of the school, big companies recruited there. IBM and Xerox even ran a training course on campus to help mold young executives, paying particular attention to Black students in their junior years. Bell was an obvious candidate and learned a lot about business when he went through the program; he wanted to pursue a career in business. This was a shock to his parents and relatives. A Black child was supposed to become a doctor or a lawyer or a minister, not a businessperson. Bell's older brother was on his way to becoming a surgeon. His twin sister would end up getting her PhD and working at NASA. Why would he ever want to go into business? But Bell had an instinct that business would open up a range of options for him, so he decided to give it a shot.

He didn't know exactly how to go about it, but a woman who worked for IBM believed in him and informally sponsored him. She helped him with his resume and cover letter, and even bought him a suit. Bell was hired and went to work in 1984 for the world's largest computer company. He expected big things to happen and new doors to open quickly.

He was gravely disappointed, and his confidence was profoundly shaken. Though he worked hard and did well, the promotions didn't come. It wasn't directly because he was Black but indirectly because of the deference and timidity he'd learned to show White people and superiors. His boss summed it up: "If we were in a foxhole, and we needed someone to get us out, you wouldn't be the guy I'd turn to. You're too nice." Bell was shaken by the assessment. He knew he wasn't "too nice," but he'd always thought that was how he was supposed to act. In fact, that niceness had been a burden to him. He'd never felt as though he could be his true self or reveal his full range of emotions. It wasn't okay to get upset, show anger, or express frustration, or even celebrate a victory and let loose once in a while. He was uncomfortable going to White people's houses. He avoided unnecessary social occasions. When the others at IBM went golfing, he said no and went to the local gym to play basketball with the kind of kids he was comfortable with growing up. He didn't realize how important all of that time on the golf course and in similar social situations was to success. He retreated from the discomfort without realizing it was part of the job.

In his first year at IBM, he failed to make the company's vaunted 100% Club for salespeople who achieved or succeeded in their annual sales quota. His second year, he failed again. In his third year, he was heading for another failure and probably the end of his career at IBM. Knowing that, he put in extra time, stayed put in the office after hours and on holidays, and tried to make his numbers someway, somehow. Out of the blue, one of his big North Carolina prospects, a man Bell had been calling on for two years to win over, suddenly submitted a hand-written purchase order for a volume so sizable that Bell went from not making his numbers to becoming one of the top four regional sales reps in the country. It was hard work that produced timely luck—and it was a game changer for Bell's career and life.

That winter he was brought to Miami and feted with the other top salespeople at the Fontainebleau Hotel. Back on the job, he started making big money as a salesperson. To accelerate his advancement, IBM sent him back to school to get his MBA at Chapel Hill. It was the hardest two years of his life. Bell was one of seven Black students in a class of 160. Only four of them made it through to graduation. During that challenging slog, Bell learned to shift his view on business from a micro-lens to a macro one. He started thinking like an executive leader, focused on cash flow, operating costs, revenue, and margins. It was a critical learning journey.

When he graduated, he followed a college roommate and went to work for the Discovery Channel in New York City. New York might have been the devil's home to his traditional Southern parents, but it was a new world of opportunity for Bell. He still had to learn how to open up, let his personality shine, and loosen up. A boss told him, "You're in the entertainment business now. You need to double your expenses every month." He meant that Bell was playing it too safe, trying not to rock the boat, being the good employee by keeping his entertainment budget down. Instead, he needed to wine and dine his prospects and clients. He needed to take risks. With those kinds of messages in his ear, Bell found his footing. It was a great time in the history of television to be in cable TV. The industry was exploding. He left Discovery for the Home and Garden Television (HGTV) channel because he had an instinct that a new venture would yield even more opportunity. He was right, and the opportunities kept coming. Soon, he was invited to join HGTV headquarters in Knoxville, Tennessee, on a path to top leadership.

The city of Knoxville had a reputation as a different kind of enclave, one for Whites, not Blacks. But Bell had a great experience there. HGTV was the biggest fish in a small pond. The co-founder and CEO, Ken Lowe, was strongly focused on developing a family culture. He spent a lot of time talking to his people and hosting events that brought in outsiders to stimulate discussions and new ideas. He also had different departments present to each other as a way of creating a broader, macro understanding of the business. Bell got a lot out of the company and its high-growth trajectory. The startup bug bit him hard, and he began to invest in real estate. After a few years, he looked around for another high-growth opportunity and took a job in Silicon Valley at a company similar to Apple TV. It was the year 2000. With head-spinning speed, the NASDAQ crashed and the company went under. Suddenly, Bell was out of a job and had no prospects or opportunities for something else.

It took a couple of hard years to get back on his feet. During that time, he moved back in with his parents. They were in poor health, so the move home made sense, but it also contributed to Bell's feeling that he'd stumbled badly. His confidence was shot. But, once again, the opportunities eventually returned. At long last, he had a chance to return to work at Discovery or join the Discovery president at a new venture, TV One. Bell chose the new venture.

The Discovery president was Johnathan Rodgers, one of the most successful Black TV executives in the history of America. Rodgers launched TV One on Martin Luther King Day in 2004. It was a cable channel targeting African American audiences in direct competition with BET. Bell was one of the founding team members and led their sales and marketing efforts before eventually becoming senior vice president. The pace of growth was phenomenal. The company reached profitability ahead of schedule. It was also Bell's first experience in a majority Black environment. The talent level blew him away, but just as importantly, Rodgers created an environment where people, specifically Black people, could be themselves. The kitchen served food from their culture. The conversations, humor, and energy made Bell feel safe to be his true self. Authenticity and diversity were prized, not as a human resources edict but because they were valuable for the business. For Bell, his colleagues, and their clients, TV One was another enclave for learning, growing, and taking risks.

The capstone of their first season was coverage of the Democratic Convention in 2008. Barack Obama was the nominee. TV One filled the week's programming with Black entertainers, like Stevie Wonder, Aretha Franklin, and John Legend, and interviewed dozens of Black leaders and politicians. After Hillary Clinton gave the speech to officially nominate Obama, a Black family stood on stage before the arena crowd. It was TV One that broadcast the production to America. They were front and center again at Grant Park in Chicago when President Obama gave his acceptance speech.

Bell's experiences at a Black company—from the market to the board room—gave him a different view of business. He now understood the potential for social change and impact, and realized he had more to share about leadership. They weren't easy lessons to digest, and the path wasn't completely straight. But in 2017, he returned to Chapel Hill as the entrepreneur-in-residence at the school's Shuford Program in Entrepreneurship to reengage with new ventures. He brought all his hard-earned experience to this new enclave, where he could help guide young people with their startups, Black students among them.

When Bell took over as executive director of the program, he started the process of figuring out which companies he could best help. From 48 Black-founded, -owned, and -operated companies, he selected seven across a diverse range of markets. He's since been using his network from Silicon Valley to New York to help them raise money, open doors, and gain access to opportunities that otherwise would have taken them a lot longer. The goal is to see these new ventures become viable businesses, then scale the program to a larger cohort.

The Ongoing Benefits of Educational Enclaves

Bernard Bell introduced co-author John Bamforth to his young friend, Nehemiah Stewart, early in Bamforth's time at UNC. Stewart was just finishing up his undergraduate degree and about to embark on his MD/PhD. At the age of 24, Stewart had two for-profit startups and a nonprofit startup under his belt.[6] Although Stewart and Bell frequently commune to solve the social problems of the day with entrepreneurship, Stewart's upbringing could not have been more different than Bell's.

Stewart is currently a medical student in the esteemed MD-PhD program at UNC-Chapel Hill, where he is completing a PhD in neuroscience before heading to residency for neurosurgery. Stewart's path to Chapel Hill was an extremely unlikely one. He was born in Prince George County, Maryland, but raised in a rough neighborhood in southeast Washington, DC, a community that has its challenges with poverty, violence, and high incarceration rates. As a child, Stewart's mother recognized her son's curiosity and dreamed for him and his brother to one day attend college—an achievement that none in their family had accomplished before. Therefore, when Stewart began schooling, his mother sent him to a majority-White high school in his grandmother's county, far from his home but with great teachers and facilities. Although a few of his cousins attended the same school, Stewart's life at home and school were vastly different. Stewart and his cousins would often be called racial slurs and were frequently accused of being "bussing" students intentionally brought to the school to help its sports teams. To make matters worse for the boys, most of the custodians at the school were related to Stewart and his cousins, so at times they were asked to help clean the school, much to the delight of their classmates. It was not uncommon for fellow students (and even teachers) to refer to the boys as "future custodians" and laugh at the boys' dreams of college. That is, until Stewart met Mrs. McGonigal, a sophomore chemistry teacher who recognized Stewart's innate talent for mathematics and encouraged him to attend college.

Stewart didn't know how he could pull that off, but he had his own enclave—his church—where members in the congregation knew he was smart and advocated for him to go to college. Stewart had no idea where to apply. Yale was the same as the University of Maryland in his view, but he was good at basketball, and UNC-Chapel Hill had an outstanding basketball program, producing, among other greats, the legendary Michael Jordan. Stewart applied to the school and got a spot on the junior varsity team, a development team for players to build critical skills and earn the chance to play with the national championship varsity team.

Stewart double majored in chemistry and mathematics and graduated with the Venable Award as the highest-achieving undergraduate student in the chemistry department for his academic performance and research accomplishments. While completing his bachelor's degree, Stewart competed for two years on the junior varsity team before being invited to work as a direct practice player for the varsity team. In addition, Stewart began completing sophisticated research on an innovative Alzheimer's project, and would ultimately publish papers in mathematics, chemistry, and neuroscience before he graduated. Everything seemed like smooth sailing until, in his second year of undergrad, his grandmother contracted terminal lung cancer, and Stewart was unable to afford a bus or plane ticket home to visit her. Stewart's frustration built into explicit anger as he realized that his inability to find transportation would force him to miss his first Thanksgiving away from home.

As he sat alone in his dorm, Stewart realized that many students driving home would advertise the open seats of their car on social media; however, students seeking rides failed to connect with drivers. He began to wonder why there was no service or app to connect riders and drivers in a university for medium-distance ridesharing, competing with Greyhound buses or the Amtrak train to destinations not too far away. While sitting alone in his dorm, he noticed an offer of a ride on a social media platform and figured there must be other drivers and riders out there who could match up. Why didn't such a service exist?

Stewart became intent on developing his idea for an app into a service and maybe even a business. But he didn't know how to go about it. Where could he get funding and advice? He had no network or contacts, but he had determination. He emailed 376 faculty members at the school who had a connection with business or entrepreneurship and asked for a 30-minute meeting. He received a "yes" from 193 of them. While faculty members were willing to give advice, no one offered any financial backing.

Eventually, Stewart met with Bernard Bell. Bell was extremely busy, now the director of a flourishing entrepreneurship program at the university, and had little time for Stewart originally. Stewart brought ideas and energy, but so did every other founder. So Bell advised him to meet with another dozen individuals who advised him to create a strong sketch mockup of what this service would look like. His conversations generated interest on campus, and he began recruiting students who wanted such a service. He also taught himself to code and worked with a bright graduate student at the University of Arizona to develop a rudimentary app. Feedback on the app was overwhelmingly positive, inspiring Stewart to take the next step and get it professionally developed. But that would take money, $40,000, and despite all the networking he'd done, he still didn't have any funding sources.

In the startup world, $40,000 might not seem like a lot, but it was almost as much as Stewart's mother made in a year. He looked into loans but could only get about $13,000. He won a pitch competition that earned him $5,000, but he was still short. By this time, hundreds of people had downloaded the app, and it was well proven, but he still couldn't get any traction with investors, even as he saw other entrepreneurs secure all the money they needed. He finally went to his mother and grandmother to ask them for the remaining $22,000. He told them he wouldn't have asked for money if he wasn't sure he could make the business work. They agreed to take out loans and lend him what he needed.

When the app was finally developed and ready, no one signed up for the first four months. The next time he saw his mother, she gently asked how the investment was working and whether she would get her money back soon. Stewart felt like he had let her down and could have begun crying. Instead, as they rode in silence, he said a prayer. He got a phone call an hour later from an alumnus who'd heard about his app, had helped launch other such companies, and wanted to invest. He asked Stewart how much he needed. Stewart answered $40,000, and recouped all the money he owed in one call.

With that money and the app, Stewart started to get traction. Students registered. User numbers picked up. His business was named one of the top 10 startups in North Carolina, and he won a Global Student Award, which gave him the opportunity to go to Silicon Valley and pitch his idea to new investors. He had limited success in Silicon Valley, except that he picked up an angel investor. He bootstrapped the company until he had six angel investors. Today, the app is called Vector Rideshare, and his company is SchoolPool, LLC. At the company's peak, Stewart managed over 50 interns and five employees (part time and full time). The business had scaled across 100 schools. During the pandemic, Stewart switched his model away from individual rides to provide subscription services to corporations and churches with the idea of helping those in rural areas travel to nearby cities or vice versa. In 2020, the platform was purchased by Lacuna.

COVID hit, then George Floyd was murdered, and in the confusing and tumultuous aftermath, the UNC administration turned to Stewart for his advice on how to work on the racial and institutional challenges that Black and Brown students faced in securing a higher education. Though he was surprised to get the call, Stewart certainly understood some of those challenges firsthand, and he channeled his own frustrations and insights into an idea for a social entrepreneurial organization he called Level the Playing Field. This time, Stewart found traction for his idea from the outset, and he had a home working out of Bernard Bell's entrepreneurship program offices where he tapped Bell's know-how, network, and support. Starting in June 2020, Stewart began working with academic and business partners across the country to establish a program to support students in HBCUs with professional skill development training and internship placements in top corporations. In a sense, he created an enclave for students like himself.

Stewart's still at UNC but now he's a third-year medical student in the NIH-funded MD-PhD program. His research passion is in the overlap of neuroscience and electrochemistry, where he's studying neurodegenerative diseases and developing new electrochemical therapeutics. While Stewart's brilliance and determination seem obvious now, his path to academics and entrepreneurship was no sure thing. He needed a great deal of support to make it to college at all, and then he needed almost unimaginable determination to get his first entrepreneurial venture off the ground. He looks back at his effort and deems it a very inefficient use of time and energy. The idea did not need to be tested across hundreds of interviews and pitches. There should have been easier ways to get backing and support, even for an idea that might ultimately not succeed. Access to opportunities, resources, and connections can have an immeasurable impact.

How many more Nehemiah Stewarts have failed to get their prayers answered while worried about paying back their mother? Fortunately, there are others bringing their entrepreneurial talents, insights, and networks to academic settings.

The Unlikely Entrepreneur

Joel Wiggins went to North Carolina A&T, one of the storied HBCUs, but he developed a strong disdain for academic courses during his time at the school.[7] Joel admitted that he was as surprised as anyone to find himself back at NC A&T as its executive director and entrepreneur-in-residence at the Center of Excellence in Entrepreneurship and Innovation, where he coached and advised minority entrepreneurs. Despite being one of the most outspoken and unlikely figures on a university campus, he was all the more effective and impactful as a coach and advisor of entrepreneurship because of his desire to teach people the unvarnished truth of what it takes to succeed.

Wiggins was born in the town of Kinston, North Carolina, about two hours from Chapel Hill. At a very young age, he tried to solve a mystery: Why weren't the Black people in his community thriving financially? He saw firsthand how hard they worked, many in the cotton and tobacco fields and warehouses. The people he knew had solid moral character. Wiggins's father was just such a person—he worked hard and played by the rules. He was, in fact, the town's first Black police officer. Wiggins's mother not only did most of the housework and child-raising, but she also worked in a factory.

In comparison, however, Wiggins noticed that the other minority group in his community, the Jewish families he considered White, were clearly more prosperous because they owned their own businesses. How did that happen? Wiggins was only six years old, but he wanted to know why circumstances were so different between two groups in the same neighborhoods. So, he actually visited with those business owners, men who owned shirt factories or stores, and talked to them. It must have surprised them to have a young person grill them about how they'd gotten their start and what it took to own a business and succeed at running it. But they treated Wiggins with respect and seemed to enjoy sharing their insights and perspectives. What struck him the most was their sense of freedom as business owners. They weren't beholden to anyone but themselves.

Wiggins noticed one other major distinction. He'd spent a lot of time around the people who worked in the fields and warehouses, listening to the stories that bound them together, and he realized now that there was a kind of victimhood to their talk that he didn't hear from the business owners. The African Americans he knew were great storytellers and conversationalists, but they seemed stuck on the same topics every day, with little sense of enthusiasm for the future or what they could do to make their lives better. The business owners had a very different mindset. They talked as though they were in control of their own circumstances, win or lose, and they focused a lot on how they would solve problems and what they could do to grow their businesses or improve their circumstances. Wiggins decided that was the mindset he wanted to adopt, and that decision shaped his life.

He started his own business on his 11th birthday. It was a lawn-cutting service. He needed other people to cut enough lawns to make it a real business, so he hired a couple of seniors in high school for help and to drive him around. He marketed his services door-to-door in more affluent and predominantly White neighborhoods, despite warnings that he would be treated with suspicion as a Black person. He found the opposite. The people who opened their doors to him were friendly, open-minded, and impressed by his pitch. Wiggins promised he'd make their lawns look immaculate, and a lot of those families were willing to hire his company on the spot. Wiggins kept up his end of the deal. He was a taskmaster who wanted the lawns done carefully and precisely, and he fired anyone who wouldn't do the job right. He welcomed the high standards his customers held him to. He wanted to be a high-standards guy.

Despite his success, he didn't get a lot of recognition or praise for his accomplishments in his own community. He wondered if that meant there was something wrong with him. The people in his community celebrated pastors, athletes, and entertainers, not business owners. In fact, they looked down on business. Wiggins had no interest in that attitude. He already knew that business ownership was an achievable path to success, and it was one that he could analyze, reverse engineer, and follow.

In junior high and high school, Wiggins leaned into his ability to work hard and hustle. He became the guy who could make money off anything. He would buy packages of candy for 10 cents and then sell each wrapped piece individually to double or triple his profits. He hired other students to

THE ENCLAVE OF EDUCATION

work for him. Confidence was never a problem. He was learning by doing. He loved figuring out how to make things happen. And he loved the feeling of success that came with it.

In contrast, he felt like he learned very little in the classroom. He was impatient with subjects that had little relevance to the real world. Wiggins studied life and how things worked, constantly looking for ways to improve himself. He observed, for example, that some people were very disciplined in their life habits while others weren't. The disciplined people chose better-quality food in the cafeteria, sat straighter at their desks, spoke more clearly, and studied harder. They also seemed to be the ones who were excelling at school. Some of those people were White. To Wiggins's friends, there was nothing to be gained by admiring or emulating a White person. But Wiggins strongly disagreed. He was on a quest to learn from anyone who could teach him how to have a more effective, productive, and successful life.

By the time he graduated from high school, he had enough money to live independently. The very next day, he moved out of his parents' house. It wasn't because he came from a bad home, but because he wanted to be his own man. It was time for him to take ownership of his life. He moved to Raleigh for the summer and got an apartment in a middle-class neighborhood and a job at a Harris Teeter grocery store where his cousin was general manager. Once again, he studied the habits of the people around him. He noticed how many middle-class people ran every day for fitness, walked their dogs, and took nice care of their lawns. He wanted that too. He even started visiting the homes of well-off friends just to see how they lived. He admired the orderliness and cleanliness he found, and the way their parents seemed to be building something for themselves, and never stuck in a life they didn't want to live.

That fall, he started school at North Carolina A&T, the only college he knew anything about, and enrolled in agriculture sciences. He quickly noticed how the world revolved around the football team on campus, so he began to approach the players and offered to get or sell them whatever they needed. Their requests ranged from clothes to weed, but whatever they wanted Wiggins would supply. He became known as the guy to turn to. He didn't stop with the football team. He studied everyone he met on campus, trying to figure out how they spent their money and whether there was an opportunity to step in and fill those needs. He noticed, for example, that people tended to spend a lot of money on alcohol on payday. So, he would stock his car and sell booze from the parking lot of the grocery store on the last day of every month. In those days, he was willing to do anything if it paid.

Another big idea was the homecoming weekend. It was clearly the most popular event on campus, and every year people were desperate to get tickets. In an effort to control the supply, Wiggins pooled all his resources and bought as many advance tickets as possible. He sold those tickets in the lead-up to the event, pleased with how the prices kept going up. By homecoming weekend, Wiggins was earning five times the original price. He stood on the steps of the dance hall and sold ticket after ticket. He didn't have to worry about anyone stopping him. He'd already paid the security guard $500 to let him conduct business without any hassle.

Once again, classroom learning seemed like a waste of time compared to what he was learning on the street. He figured there had to be something worth studying at college, though. The business students were more his style, so he decided to look into transferring into their department. He made an appointment with the dean's office to ask about entrepreneurial studies. The dean told him there was no such thing. Wiggins could study business management, marketing, or accounting. Once again, Wiggins felt like his time in class was a waste, as anything related to entrepreneurship felt purposely left out. He'd need to learn that elsewhere.

He continued his studies, but he still wanted to build a business. How were students spending their money? On clothes. What if he could get fashionable brands at a good price? He worked out a distribution deal with a popular brand to sell clothes on campus, but they turned him down because he was only 18 years old. So, Wiggins got a job at a clothing store for a similar reason: He could get a 50 percent employee discount. After each weekly paycheck, he'd buy a bunch of suits and sell them at a profit.

Wiggins soon had a reputation within the department. It was not entirely good but not entirely bad either. They could see and appreciate his hustle, but they also feared it and wished it was better directed. Nearing graduation, someone at the university suggested he interview with the Ford Motor Company, which had representatives on campus. Wiggins was dubious about a company he considered to be run by and for "good old boys." But he decided to give it a shot. The interviewer was a Black woman, someone Wiggins instinctively understood. When she asked him about his ability to multitask and project plan, Wiggins asked her if she liked to cook. Then he went into a detailed description of the ordered way he shopped for groceries, prepared his meals, and conducted his life. Won over by his earnestness and his impressive determination to make something of himself, she recommended him for advancement.

In fact, he was one of several hundred people selected to go through the next round of interviews. Only a few would be chosen by Detroit. He was competing against the best and the brightest from Ivy League schools. After another grueling round, Wiggins got a call from Ford corporate headquarters. Not only did they want to offer him a job, but they also told him he'd achieved the highest score ever. So much for the Ivy Leaguers. He'd learned more from doing than those students had learned in class. Now Ford knew it, too.

His early experiences at Ford corporate reinforced his belief that real-world entrepreneurial experience was more valuable than classroom learning. Within six months, he was promoted to market representative manager and began to work directly with dealership owners around the country. Wiggins enjoyed the dealers. He loved walking the floor with them and seeing how they kept tabs on the complex, multifaceted business of successfully running a dealership. The owners recognized a kindred spirit in him. They could tell he wasn't meant to be a corporate guy. He thought and behaved differently. He began to get consistent messages that he should come over to the other side. Still, Wiggins was the number-one performing Ford employee for 42 months running. He was getting messages from corporate, too; they valued him and thought he was executive material.

Then, Wiggins met a dealer who finally tipped the balance. The two clashed from the start. The dealer was one of the most successful in the country, but he was a bully. He had once been with corporate and knew how decisions were made, and he used that knowledge to his advantage, coercing representatives into doing his bidding. Wiggins was not one to be cowed and knew he had the power in the relationship. When the dealer demanded that Wiggins give him more inventory than he was allocated, Wiggins refused and wouldn't back down, even when the dealer threatened to call Alex Trotman, the CEO . . . and his friend. Wiggins told him to go ahead. The dealer finally laughed. Wiggins was the first rep in 25 years who had ever stood up to him.

Wiggins opened up in turn. He told the dealer that he hated the corporate world, but he needed time to learn how it worked and do all the networking possible. That was his excuse for not taking the leap. And secretly, Wiggins was a little worried, too. Unlike most of the dealer-owners, he was not from generational wealth. But he also understood the game of business very well. He knew it required resilience, strength, and timing. Soon, he would be ready.

The sign it was time arrived in the form of a Pennsylvania-based dealer named Fred Beans, who was considered one of the best in the nation. All of his lots were extremely profitable. One of Beans's senior guys approached Wiggins and offered him a job on the team. Wiggins replied that he wasn't a "work-for type guy." But the question kicked up a lot of feelings. He wanted to learn from someone like Beans. The problem was, he had just been offered a big promotion by corporate. He knew the promotion path wasn't right for him. He hadn't been happy when he heard the offer, he'd been pissed, though his face showed no emotion. As promising as the corporate path might be, he felt like it was too limiting. He returned a week later and told them he would work for Beans instead. They were shocked. Why would he throw away an opportunity like this? Wiggins didn't flinch. For him, it wasn't about the money or the prestige. He was driven by a desire to know what he could do. This time Beans came back to him with an offer that provided a path to ownership of his own dealership one day.

Wiggins went to work for Beans as a general manager. The dealership was in a town that was 99 percent White. As a rep, Wiggins had been told to be out of the area after sundown. He didn't care. He started learning about the business like drinking out of a fire hose. He worked his tail off, coming in early and leaving late. No matter what, no one was going to outwork him. Beans saw it. Soon, he offered Wiggins an opportunity to buy one of his dealerships with Beans's son as a partner. Wiggins would only do it if he could be the majority owner.

Corporate was skeptical he could make the numbers work and pay Fred Beans off, given the dealership's current performance. Wiggins told them they were crazy. He knew he could. He bought Fred Beans out in 10 years. Two-and-a-half years after that, he had four more dealerships. Finally, he had achieved a level of success that felt like he'd arrived.

Today, Wiggins recognizes that many African Americans have a disadvantage when it comes to running a business: They don't come from second- or third-generation business owners. The shift from an employee mindset to an ownership mindset was the biggest change in the next stage of Wiggins's entrepreneurial journey.

To learn how to lead his business from an ownership mindset, Wiggins learned to ask himself, "What would Fred Beans do?" For example, Beans taught Wiggins and his people to analyze financial performance in percentages, not dollars. That made a huge impact on Wiggins. Beans was teaching him to think like an owner, not a dealer. Regardless of how much money a location made, decisions about performance, inventory, resource deployment, and asset utilization were always clearer with relative scores.

There was also a rhythm to the way Beans handled the day-to-day. Beans would visit a store and carefully survey the parking lot, driving up and down every aisle. Then, he would enter through the back entrance to get a full view of the shop. He was looking for order. He wanted to see how his processes were being put into action. In meetings with his key people, Beans was precise and asked pointed questions that demonstrated that he really understood each person's specific job. He also had a view of the organization that included how all the different roles fit together and how to talk to individual employees so they understood how their work impacted the organization as a whole. He knew what reports to read and how to analyze the numbers.

Wiggins brought his own skills to the table, too: his incredible attention to detail, his savviness with understanding people, and the edge he had coming from the street, not family money. He connected with people differently and paid more attention to the employees in the shop or the back, people Beans might have spent less time on. He gave his shop people more authority over their corner of the dealership and more incentive to improve their performance. Wiggins didn't want to be a cookie-cutter owner or another guy from corporate. He knew what it was like to be bullied or talked down to, and he knew how to treat people so they felt respected and noticed.

When Wiggins's stores began to stand out for their performance numbers, other dealers around the country showed up to study how he did it.

Within a few years of having established himself as a premier owner, Wiggins began to diversify. The more success he had in the car business, the more bored he got. He considered his success a byproduct of focus and drive. It had little to do with liking cars (which he does not). Like a lot of entrepreneurs, he got more juice from figuring out a new business and launching it than from running it.

He started a car-related marketing business called Change and Rotation, aimed at helping dealers with profitability. Change and Rotation developed the idea of incentivizing customers to come back to the dealership for maintenance over the first 18 months. It helped increase parts sales and customer retention, and is now standard practice in the industry, but Wiggins put the wrong people in charge and didn't give the business a fighting chance to succeed. He knows it could have been an extremely lucrative venture.

Wiggins tried other business ideas. He liked clothing, which was a high-margin business. But he didn't think much of the service he received as a customer. So, he began to put his mind to how he might operate such a business differently and opened a number of stores.

He began to think about the impact business could have on the community. He noticed that it wasn't the churches and nonprofits doing the most good in the community, it was the business owners sitting on the boards funding programs and services. He realized that to impact the community in a better way, he should be doing it as a businessperson, not a pastor or nonprofit director. So, he started Celebrate Family, which is the largest outdoor dance in Raleigh, North Carolina. And he created other businesses to support entrepreneurs and business leaders, like the Kingmaker Program, which he and his wife developed to teach business to people of color. His first group of students varied in age from 18 to 70. He taught them how to hold themselves to the highest standards in conducting business, show discipline in their work, and have confidence in the innovation power of their ideas. They had more ideas than most people he worked with. One woman who cleaned houses launched her own maid service and soon had 40 people working for her.

It all came full circle when he was invited back to his alma mater, North Carolina A&T State University, as an entrepreneur-in-residence. He returned because they asked him to bring an entrepreneurial mindset to campus. That's what he had wanted all those years ago.

Wiggins told the president that he would need to shake things up to make that happen. And to the administration's credit, they signed on. A week later, they asked him to help put together a board that could support the kind of program he had in mind. Once again, he told them that they might not like how he did that because his board would be entrepreneurs, not academics.

Studying the inherent conflict between entrepreneurship and the big institution of academia, he thought of how much the administration focused on fundraising, erecting new buildings, and starting new programs that would draw students and still more funding. And he suddenly realized something fundamental. The most under-utilized resource on campus was the students themselves. The COVID shutdown only reinforced his new awareness that people and programs mattered more than buildings and classroom learning. He started talking to the administration about student potential in a different way. He told them that he didn't need buildings to educate and train the next generation. He needed their greatest assets, which were their students, the very people they were overlooking, just as they had overlooked him 30 years earlier. In his mind, the best output of the university was not students with good grades, but students who are set up to realize their full potential.

When Wiggins developed his entrepreneurship program on campus, that's what he told the students who signed on. His job over four years would be to make sure they were fully prepared when they left to succeed. That meant shaping their souls, their will, and their minds through discipline, self-regulation, and exposure to opportunity. He knew that could take many forms of learning. One way he wanted to broaden horizons was to bring students who didn't ordinarily have the chance to travel abroad to see some of the world. So, he brought his first cohort of entrepreneurs-in-training to Italy. Another way was by bringing classroom speakers who did not look or sound like academics but had important perspectives to convey. He knew that entrepreneurship couldn't be taught like classroom learning, it needed to be felt, experienced, and practiced. It wasn't about theory or raising money or even networking, but about sitting across from someone and figuring out what made them tick. And building relationships. And earning people's trust. And having the courage and conviction to knock on doors and jump on opportunities. He knew that finding money or coming up with ideas wasn't the hard part anymore; it was developing the necessary mindset. Wiggins wanted to train people to think like owners and lose the belief that they need anyone else to do something for them.

Soon, students and faculty noticed the different energy he was bringing to campus. In an environment that rewarded a certain kind of conformity, he was a new kind of role model—an innovator and entrepreneur. Like others we'll describe, Wiggins is one of many innovative investors who see the untapped potential of HBCUs and are helping students think more like entrepreneurs and owners, following paths that involve more risk but potentially more reward.

4

THE OWNERSHIP IMPERATIVE

The Rondo neighborhood of St. Paul, Minnesota, was an enclave for Black residents of the predominantly White state. Home to Black-owned grocery stores, car dealerships, repair shops, tailors, barbershops, churches, restaurants, social clubs, community centers, music halls, a newspaper, and even a baseball team, the middle-class neighborhood had thrived as a center for Black culture, business, and wealth since the late 1800s. The foundation of that wealth—the reason why it was spread so broadly—was home ownership. Many families in the neighborhood owned their own homes and were able to pass on that form of wealth to their children.

The Federal-Aid Highway Act of 1956 ended all that. The chosen route for a new highway cut straight through the heart of Rondo. To build the highway, the state seized homes and businesses under eminent domain and destroyed them. Businesses and homeowners who resisted were met with physical violence. The new six-lane highway divided the neighborhood in half, devastating its cultural and social cohesion, its economic vibrancy, and even its environment with the uptick in pollution and its long-term impact on health. Displaced residents spread out to new neighborhoods, including Frog Town, the curiously named nearby neighborhood that counts with Rondo among the poorest in Minneapolis–St. Paul today.

Ownership is imperative to generational wealth. If the goal is to catalyze and accelerate the kind of wealth creation that can support and sustain economic growth and social empowerment over generations, then wealth alone is not enough. Ownership is critical.

For many, that means owning a home. As the residents of Rondo can attest, the loss of that ownership has generational consequences. But the kind of wealth that can foster and stimulate innovation and entrepreneurship comes through the ownership of businesses, non-primary real estate, stocks, and intellectual property. This kind of ownership can compound wealth and broaden its impact, allowing for new acquisitions and reinvestment. It even serves as collateral for gaining access to additional capital at lower interest rates, creating more flexibility and financial power. It can also create the kind of security that fosters risk-taking in many forms.

Today, most wealth in America is concentrated in the ownership class. In 2023, the top 10 percent of the wealthiest people in the country held 66 percent of the nation's total wealth. The top 1 percent held 26.5 percent. For Black Americans, entry into that ownership class has been challenging, given the relative paucity of inherited wealth. Among the paths available, sports and entertainment stand out.

The Fight of the Century

Joe Louis was born poor in rural Alabama to parents who were the children of former slaves. He would die poor, too, owing more in taxes than he could pay. He got by at the end of his life, working at Caesars Palace in Las Vegas as "host-in-residence," shaking hands with guests who were thrilled to meet the former heavyweight boxing champion. Louis's inability to leverage his fame into financial success and lasting wealth is striking in this era when star athletes can earn even more money outside their sport than on the field or in the ring. Louis's personal and business missteps compounded the societal barriers he faced to achieving entrepreneurial success, even as an American hero and one of the most famous people in the world.

There was little possibility of success and prosperity for a Black man in Alabama in the early 1900s. With the resurgence of the KKK and the discriminatory policies, laws, and social mores of Jim Crow, Black communities were under siege. Louis's family moved north in 1926 as part of the first Great Migration. They settled in a predominantly Black neighborhood in Detroit after Louis's older brother got a job at the Ford Motor Company. The world's largest auto manufacturer was considered progressive at that time because Black workers received the same five-dollar-a-day wage as Whites.

Joe Louis's success as an amateur boxer led him to turn pro. As he continued to rack up wins and rise in the rankings, his handlers crafted an image of an affable, wholesome brute, intriguing, enthralling, and palatable to the White media and fan base. In 1935, as the number-one contender for the world heavyweight boxing title, he was named the Associated Press's Athlete of the Year. In 1937, he finally won the heavyweight title after defeating James Braddock in a brutal knockout. But it was his title defense against Max Schmeling in 1938 that made Joe Louis an icon.

Schmeling had defeated Louis two years earlier. Though Schmeling was not a Nazi, his victory over Louis had made him a hero in Nazi Germany, a man Adolf Hitler praised as a symbol of Aryan purity.[1] Given his earlier loss to Schmeling, Louis had his reasons for wanting to beat the German, but the political pressure he felt was even stronger. Before the bout, President Franklin Delano Roosevelt met with Louis and told him the nation was counting on him to defeat "Germany" in the ring.[2]

The "fight of the century" took place at Yankee Stadium and was broadcast by radio around the world. The victory was resounding. Louis forced Schmeling to throw in the towel before the end of the first round. Louis was applauded and appreciated by Whites for defeating the Germans, and his win unleashed joy within Black communities. The celebrations in Black neighborhoods lasted for days.

That was the peak of Louis's fame and fortune.

Though Schmeling and Louis had met in the ring, and Louis had emerged victorious, Schmeling went on to greater fortune. Louis defended his title repeatedly before America entered the war, earning his status as one of the greatest heavyweight champions ever; then he served in a special services division of the military to help raise troop morale. Despite his fame, he encountered racism at every turn, and as his winnings from boxing matches ran out, desperation began to creep in. By the end of the war, he was deep in debt to the IRS because of financial mismanagement by his handlers and forced to continue fighting long past his prime to make a living and repay the money he owed.

After finally retiring from the ring, Louis took a last swing at success. He had long wanted to open his own Ford dealership in Chicago. Since the company had helped his family make ends meet decades before, he felt a strong affinity for the brand. He met personally with the company's CEO, Henry Ford II, to ask for the opportunity to become the first Black person to own and run a Ford dealership. Ford asked his general managers to canvas opinions from dealers and general managers around the country. Reactions were unequivocally negative. Indeed, the dealers described the prospect of Louis as a Ford dealer in catastrophic terms. "The Ford business is a White man's business and we do not want any Negroes in it," one wrote. Another put it more emotionally, "The writer is bitterly against the possibility of the appointment of Negro dealers and lacks words to express his feelings against the idea." A third said, "If we wish to pioneer a principle of American democracy in business . . . it is my opinion that this is not the proper time, nor the proper party involved."[3]

Heeding those voices, Ford turned Louis down. In distinct contrast, Max Schmeling, the loser of their heavyweight bout and Hitler's favorite boxer, was awarded the Coca-Cola franchise for northern Germany after the war and became immensely rich.

Given the power of the endorsements of star athletes today, there seems little doubt that Louis would have influenced the sales of Ford cars and opened new markets to the company at a time when America's pioneering automaker had fallen to third-place status among the big three. Even today, less than 2 percent of America's Ford dealerships have a Black owner, and only 5 percent are owned by a person of any minority.

Louis did not achieve the life he imagined for himself. He started several businesses—a restaurant, an insurance company, and a hair products company, among others—but all failed. He was a generous man, beloved all his life by the public, who earned a lot more for his handlers than himself and gave away much of his remaining money to friends, family, and local communities. The debt and the physical punishment he'd experienced took their toll, and he fell into drug addiction. Friends, including Schmeling, came to his financial aid where they could, but he died without means in 1981 at age 66, after attending his last heavyweight championship bout.

The Path to Ownership Through Athletics

In contrast to Joe Louis, George Foreman managed to capitalize on his fame as a two-time World Heavyweight Boxing Champion and achieve significant wealth. Foreman grew up poor and rough in Houston but applied his amateur boxing abilities to win a gold medal at the 1968 Olympics in Mexico City. Turning pro, he went on a remarkable run of wins, most of them by knockout, before becoming the World Heavyweight Champion during the period when Muhammad Ali was banned from the sport for his refusal to serve in the Vietnam War. The two fighters finally met in the ring in Zaire, in 1974, in the match known as the Rumble in the Jungle. After Foreman lost in a stunning defeat, his life went downhill. More losses followed, and after one particularly bad knockout, he experienced a religious epiphany upon waking up in his dressing room. He immediately retired from the sport and became a preacher. He also opened up with the public and revealed a transformed personality. Once infamous for a gruff, severe demeanor with few words for anyone, Foreman became a gregarious, friendly, outspoken charmer who won over everyone he met.

As a minister, Foreman devoted himself to developing community support programs for troubled youth. But now he faced a problem familiar to many former superstar athletes. Despite the tens of millions he'd earned fighting, he was running out of money, and his resources were insufficient to fund his programs. "I was going to go broke the Joe Louis route," Foreman acknowledged. "So, I decided to box again."[4]

At age 40, after a decade out of the ring and looking to any observer like an overweight and out-of-shape has-been, his comeback was considered unlikely at best. But Foreman took on his opponents with gusto. Notably, he showed remarkable stamina in late rounds, winning bout after bout by outlasting his adversaries. He credited his success in the ring to healthy eating. This repeated refrain made him a great spokesperson for a new kitchen appliance—an indoor grill tilted at an angle to reduce fat. Foreman pitched the George Foreman Grill with the same zest he had shown in his return to the ring. He also secured himself one of the greatest endorsement deals of all time. As the George Foreman Grill flew off the shelves, George Foreman earned 40 percent of the profits on each unit sold, around $4.5 million per month at its peak. By the time he finally sold out his interest, Foreman had earned an estimated $200 million. He also served as super-spokesperson for other companies, including Meineke, the muffler company, and launched a variety of his own products and services, including a line of environmentally safe cleaning products, a shoe for diabetics, personal care products, several best-selling books, a health shake, and a restaurant franchise. The lesson of Joe Louis was not lost on George Foreman.

Other Black athletes learned these lessons, too. In the 1970s, as George Foreman entered his boxing hiatus, the National Basketball Association reached the nadir of its popularity. Despite a slew of players who are now legendary for their talent, the league was perceived as too slow, too rough, and too Black for mainstream America. This resulted in low television ratings, poor attendance, and championship games shown on tape delay. In 1979, the electrifying talent and irresistible charisma of the rookie Magic Johnson helped turn the league's fortunes around.

Despite growing up in modest means in Detroit, Johnson knew his worth. He negotiated one of the highest rookie contracts ever, threatening to go back to school if the Lakers didn't meet his demands. Then, he began fielding offers from corporations, especially shoe companies, eager to benefit from his endorsement. One of those shoe companies was Nike, a newcomer in the world of sports apparel, armed with technically innovative designs and co-founder Phil Knight, one of the greatest marketers in history. Unlike other shoe company representatives vying for Johnson, Knight did not want to negotiate a flat fee. He wanted a brand co-sponsor, someone whose earnings would be tied to the company's growth. In his proposal, Johnson would get his own line of Nike shoes, plus $100,000 in Nike stock and a one-dollar royalty for every Nike Magic shoe sold. Johnson turned down the deal for a cash offer of $100,000 from Converse. "I didn't know anything about stock," Johnson later explained. "I'm from the inner city."

If Johnson had signed with Nike, that stock and royalty offer could have been worth over $5 billion by some estimates.

Nineteen-year-old Magic Johnson may not have known anything about stock, but Michael Jordan, who followed Johnson as the next Black superstar, learned very quickly. At UNC-Chapel Hill Jordan had made the national championship-winning basket as a freshman and turned pro two years later, going third overall in the NBA draft of 1984. Today, he is considered the greatest basketball player of all time on the court, but he has earned more than any professional athlete ever, off the court. Over his 13-year playing career, Jordan earned around $94 million in salary, most of that in his final two years. But it was the endorsements that kick-started his real wealth. Before his NBA playing days officially began, Jordan's mother convinced him to go with Nike over Adidas, pushing his agents and Nike to negotiate a ground-breaking endorsement deal on his behalf. That deal included $2.5 million in cash and his own line of shoes with a royalty on each shoe sold. The shoes were so different in style and function that the NBA fined Jordan $5,000 a game for wearing them that first year. Nike paid the fine on Jordan's behalf, happy to receive all the free advertising that accrued from the league's ongoing battle against the shoe and the game's greatest star.

The Air Jordan brand became a standalone business for Nike, earning billions a year in revenue, and likely netting Jordan over one hundred million each year in royalties. Jordan also endorsed a variety of other products, ranging from Coca-Cola to Gatorade, Chevrolet, McDonald's, Wheaties, and Hanes, among others. He has fostered other investments in restaurants, car dealerships, and assorted businesses. But it was his ownership of the NBA's Charlotte Hornets that brought Jordan's wealth to another level. Jordan had long shown interest in NBA ownership, taking a minority stake in the Washington Wizards in his last year as a player. In 2006, he bought a minority stake in the Charlotte Bobcats (which became the Hornets in 2013), with majority owner Robert L. Johnson, the co-founder of BET (Black Entertainment Television) and the first Black billionaire. Johnson sold a majority stake to Jordan in 2010, making him the first former player to become an NBA team owner. The Hornets' value has risen precipitously in the years since. Today, Jordan's net worth is believed to be around $1.6 billion. The difference between endorsements and ownership was stunning.

Other Black athletes have followed a similar path to generational wealth through ownership, off the court, or out of the ring. As noted in Chapter 1, Serena Williams, the tennis champion, parlayed her court earnings into a fashion empire, a variety of lucrative endorsements, and some savvy business investments. David Robinson, the former San Antonio Spur and basketball great, leveraged his playing salary to launch Admiral Capital Group as his vehicle for making investments in various businesses. Tiger Woods, the golfer, has earned considerable wealth from endorsements and investments in digital tech.

Back to the NBA, Vinnie Johnson, an unheralded member of the Detroit Pistons, turned $5 million in career earnings into $400 million of net worth by founding The Piston Group, a parts supplier to auto manufacturers. Magic Johnson may have missed out on the Nike endorsement, but as a player he began to think seriously and talk to mentors about why so many athletes fail to retain their wealth and build successful businesses, determining that ownership was the key. After retiring, he launched a sporting goods store that failed after a year, but the experience taught

Johnson a great deal about listening to customers and growing a business. He began to advocate for investing in urban communities. Through Magic Johnson Enterprises, Johnson invested in movie theaters in cities across the country and a pre-paid Mastercard that could help low-income people save money and conduct e-commerce. With the support of Starbucks CEO Howard Schultz, Johnson also bought 125 Starbucks stores for urban locations, based on his view that minority neighborhoods desperately wanted such offerings. His stores earned above-average per-capita sales. Johnson also bought a PepsiCo bottling operation, the largest minority-owned facility in the United States, and he secured minority stakes in several different professional sports franchises.

Like Johnson, fellow Lakers star Shaquille O'Neal made smart use of his career earnings and endorsement deals to pour money into ownership, investing extensively in restaurant and fitness club franchises, real estate, insurance, and digital technology companies. One of his early investments was pre-IPO Google, which paid off spectacularly. O'Neal also co-founded an ad agency focused on diversity. His goal with the firm is to flip the normal diversity targets of ad agencies and "turn the minority into the majority."[5]

Most recently, NBA star LeBron James joined the billionaire athlete club, the first to do so while still an active player. He managed this by leveraging his endorsements to fund business ventures and make investments. Almost half of his wealth comes from stakes in a pizza chain, the Fenway Sports Group, and a production company.

But what about athletes who can't earn astronomical salaries and endorsements? The path to ownership works for them, too.

It's Hard to Be What You Can't See

Karen LeVert was five years old when she saw a woman with a briefcase and asked her mom what that meant. LeVert's mother explained to her that the woman carried a briefcase because she was a businesswoman. LeVert immediately told her mother that's what she wanted to be when she grew up. She often thinks back to that moment with her mother and reflects on how important it is to have visible examples of success. "It's hard to be what you can't see," she often says. Exposing others to possibility remains one of her driving interests as a business leader, entrepreneur, and venture capitalist today.[6]

Her parents were from the Deep South. Her father was born in the 1930s in a small town in Alabama. Her mother grew up in southern Georgia, with her mom, a widow, doing domestic work, including picking beans for a living. But both of LeVert's parents wanted more for themselves. LeVert's mother moved from her childhood home in Georgia to Cleveland to live with an uncle and attend nursing school. LeVert's father wanted to secure a college degree, but he couldn't enroll in a university due to racial discrimination. Instead, he entered the armed forces to use the GI Bill for his education. An extremely intelligent man, Mr. LeVert got a job with the Department of Defense (after finishing technical school), where he worked on the Minuteman Missile project. He learned as much about rocket technology as an engineer and instilled a love of science in his children. He also modeled a level of resiliency and stoicism that his daughter admired all her life—even more when she learned that he'd been a POW in Korea for almost four years. During his imprisonment, the enemy intelligence officers taunted him for showing loyalty to a country that treated Black people as second-class citizens, but he never wavered.

Karen LeVert always saw her parents remain steadfast in their goals and how they treated others. They both worked hard to give their children opportunities that had been unavailable to them. The schools in Ohio were still segregated, so the LeVerts moved to a small town where their children could receive quality education. After buying a house in a nice middle-class neighborhood, many of their White neighbors immediately put their own houses up for sale. Years later, after growing friendships in the community, those neighbors apologized for the ignorance and racism they'd demonstrated at the time.

LeVert was bright and success-oriented as a child, but in her early education, she was shunned by her new classmates at first. Like her parents, she didn't let that treatment get to her. She studied hard, earned top grades, excelled in sports, and remained cheerful and friendly to all, winning over everyone. By the time she graduated, she was class salutatorian, elected homecoming queen and to the prom court, a star athlete, and among the most popular students in school.

She went on to attend Eastern Michigan University, which her father noticed had an information technology degree where she didn't have to double major in business and computer science. She walked onto the basketball team and ultimately played all four years, earning a full scholarship. Sports was a ticket to an affordable education, though her parents had saved for their children to go to college. LeVert enrolled as a business major with a concentration in computer science. The combination wove together her father's love of science and her own goal to be a "woman with a briefcase." She played ball all four years, took tough courses, and graduated without debt. Very soon, she got a job working for Nationwide Insurance as a computer programmer.

Her initial trainer at Nationwide was not very helpful, so LeVert learned most of the training on her own. It wasn't a hardship for her, or unexpected, to encounter resistance in a new environment. But she had her parents' stoicism and shared their determination to never give up. Her perseverance and performance earned her attention from higher-ups. Many of her bosses, all White males, saw her potential and gave her a series of ever tougher and more complex assignments. The opportunities fueled her success, and she found herself on the path to becoming a top executive. In recognition of that trajectory, the company sent her to the Center for Creative Leadership in Greensboro, North Carolina, where many top high-potential leaders receive training. The experience opened LeVert's eyes to a different opportunity than her bosses at Nationwide might have expected. She discovered that she wanted to be an entrepreneur.

The entrepreneurial bug didn't go away once the training program ended, though LeVert didn't know what to do with that urge at first. She was chosen by Nationwide to run a 500-person service center in North Carolina, one of six around the country. The company also put her through business school to get an MBA, where she studied finance and entrepreneurship. The pay and recognition at such a young age were rewarding, but she was reluctant to move to the South. Her parents, after all, had left the South for opportunities in the North, and she'd spent enough time growing up visiting poor towns in Alabama and Georgia to know how hard those areas could be on minorities. But LeVert ended up taking the assignment and discovered, to her surprise, that she loved North Carolina. It was diverse, progressive, and innovative. Her parents had previously moved there, as well, as soon as her father was able to retire with full military benefits as a former prisoner of war. She bought a sailboat, something she'd always wanted since taking a sailing class in college. When Nationwide decided to transfer her to another part of the country for a new assignment, she was conflicted. Maybe this was the time to try entrepreneurship.

She asked for a leave of absence from the company to figure that out. They were reluctant, but when she told them she would quit if they didn't give her time off, they agreed. Soon, however, she encountered a different problem: What kind of entrepreneurial venture should she devote herself to? She scoured the newspaper for ideas and soon came across a franchise opportunity with a company called Environmental Biotech that sold a bacterial technology used to break down grease, sugars, and starches. LeVert was intrigued by the idea of an innovative solution immediately applicable in the market. The franchise rights were for a territory or region, so she bought the rights for three nearby counties and got to work selling the technology to restaurants. Driving her truck across the region, from restaurant to restaurant, it occurred to her more than once that she'd gone from 500 employees to one. She didn't have the strongest interest in the product, but she was attracted to the ownership aspect of having her own business. She was hungry to be independent and to make her own decisions.

She quickly realized that most restaurant owners couldn't care less about the environmental impact of putting caustic chemicals down drains, so she pivoted to hotels and corporate cafeterias. The business began to grow, but she was already interested in doing something new. In a case of good timing, a neighbor asked if he could join her or buy in. He'd watched her having fun outside the corporate world and wanted that kind of freedom and ownership for himself. So, LeVert sold part of the company to him and let him take over operations.

LeVert believes in taking time to celebrate wins, so she treated herself to a vacation at a Club Med in Mexico. While there, she met another guest named Lisa Henderson and the two got to know each other. Henderson had also been a college scholarship athlete, like LeVert, though she didn't have parents as focused on education and had only gotten a soccer scholarship because of a chance encounter. As a high school senior, she'd attended a game at a nearby college to watch her friends play. Since the team didn't have enough players, Henderson was asked to put on a jersey and join in. She scored two goals, and the coach offered her a scholarship on the spot.

That chance to go to college changed Henderson's life. She went on to get a bachelor's in finance, an athlete-of-the-year award, and an MBA. That turned into a series of good corporate jobs before she landed at Autodesk, the San Francisco–based software company. Exposure to tech in San Francisco in the late nineties was an easy way to get the startup bug. Henderson and LeVert shared that fire and began talking about Henderson's idea for an internet-based service that would give exposure to promising high school and junior college athletes to four-year colleges and universities.

LeVert signed on, joining Henderson in San Francisco to create a business plan for LevelEdge, a clearing house for athletic talent with a subscription plan business model. Investors and backers loved the idea, including retired tennis champion Billie Jean King, who became co-chair of the board, and large companies like Nike. Very quickly, LeVert and Henderson raised a dizzying sum of money, ultimately more than $10 million, without even drawing up a fully developed business plan. They could have raised even more because of all the attention and accolades. Henderson was profiled in the *New York Times*[7] and made the cover of *US News and World Report*. The company hosted a big launch party, with all of the extravagances of the dot-com era.

Soon, the company employed high-cost programmers in San Francisco, which felt expensive compared to her North Carolina experience. After launching her initial startup from her own personal funds, LeVert began to have misgivings about their burn rate and lack of revenue. However, this was a trademark dot-com business, relying on eyeballs and ad revenue for success.

Sometimes failure can be the best thing that happens to an entrepreneur. The demise of LevelEdge was inevitable once the dot-com bubble burst, but LeVert learned an important lesson about how startups succeed. Along with having strong revenue plans, cultural alignment among the founders and across the senior team is critical. Luckily, she soon met folks who aligned with her very well: Kristina Johnson and Gail Goestenkors.

The introduction came at a party held by an assistant coach of Gail Goestenkors, coach of the Duke University women's basketball team.

LeVert had played basketball against Goestenkors in college. They reconnected when LeVert pitched her at Duke on LevelEdge. Now that LevelEdge was shuttered, Goestenkors saw a potential business match between LeVert and Kristina Johnson, also a former student-athlete. Goestenkors had great ideas, LeVert had execution ability, and Johnson had a rare understanding of science and technology, plus she knew how to raise money. Johnson had launched the women's lacrosse team at Stanford. Now, she was a rising star in science and academia. Ultimately, she would serve as under secretary for energy in the Obama Administration, launch her own hydro-power energy firm, and become chancellor of SUNY before taking on an even bigger role as president of Ohio State University. Along the way, she collected a string of accolades for her engineering and science breakthroughs, inventions, and patents.

Johnson and LeVert hit it off, and the three began to share ideas for potential ventures. In her role in academia, Johnson had seen a lot of great research and untapped technology come and go. "What if we built a private tech transfer company?" The idea was not to compete against university tech transfer offices but to complement them. LeVert saw the potential right away. Together, they decided to launch an accelerator called Southeast TechInventures to support the creative ideas of academic researchers, scientists, and engineers. It was a classic approach to innovation, bringing complementary competencies together. Over the next decade, the accelerator and its spinoffs raised $50 million in funding, secured $50 million in grant funding, and achieved hundreds of millions of dollars in valuations. Investors received a five-fold return.

LeVert loves the opportunity to support innovators that she helps discover and launch. Early on, she found that she was skilled at identifying and selecting people to back. Her starting point was always the founders themselves, rather than the idea or technology they wanted to bring to market. She likes people who've experienced failure, setbacks, and tough challenges in their lives because those are the ones who know how to fight their way through difficulties and barriers. She also likes people who have corporate backgrounds because they understand processes and structures, have deeper industry networks, and know better how to navigate bureaucracy.

While commercializing early-stage technologies, LeVert noticed there was a dearth of capital at this stage. She decided to fix that problem by launching her own venture firm, LeVert Ventures. New to the venture capital (VC) world, she approached 30-year VC veteran Art Pappas to partner with on the fund. LeVert Ventures is a specialized fund of Pappas Capital. LeVert (French for *the green*) is an early-stage venture fund focused on agricultural technologies or AgTech. She chose AgTech because of the importance of food, water, and sustainable practices in the future, and because of her own past, growing up in a town where many of her classmates came from farming backgrounds. She's putting a stake in the ground in three major areas for early-stage companies: (1) precision or intelligent agriculture informed by AI, machine learning, sensors, and so on; (2) biological technologies that prevent or eliminate disease and pests; and (3) indoor or controlled-environment tech that can bring food production to cities while reducing transportation, pollution, and disease.

Even though LeVert Ventures won't be investing in solely diverse founders, LeVert is very much looking forward to having more diverse founders than most venture funds. Being open to backing the best founders makes her more likely to have a diverse portfolio. With that diversity and her own position as a Black woman, she finds that a more diverse pool of candidates approaches her, and she is not dismissive of their overtures, unlike many in the industry.

She values diversity of experience and background in startup teams, too, and encourages non-diverse groups to rethink their makeup. Entrepreneurs are in business to solve a problem, but they don't always accurately or deeply understand the problems of the market without a diverse team. LeVert also recognizes that diverse founders are held to a different level of scrutiny by decision-makers and gatekeepers. Stereotypes and biases come into play. LeVert has encountered those attitudes in fundraising and even with former board members who later apologized (one in tears) for not having the faith in her initially to run the company.

LeVert wants more autonomy and control because she loves innovation and helping early-stage companies. She also wants to build her own generational wealth. She's seen how backers with preferred stock earn the biggest and most direct returns. For LeVert, it's not about the money; it's about the question "Why not me?" That's a question that entrepreneurs and wealth creators ask themselves all the time.

Wealth Through Entertainment

Instead of the stories of Michael Jordan, Magic Johnson, Serena Williams, Tiger Woods, and others among the richest African Americans, similar stories could be told of people in the entertainment industry, such as Oprah Winfrey, Jay-Z, and Rihanna. The critical factor to real wealth, once again, is ownership.

Sheila Johnson understands this well. Born in 1949 in Pennsylvania, Johnson was the daughter of a neurosurgeon who worked for the US Veterans Administration and an accountant. Her family moved often, as her father, who was not allowed to work in White hospitals or conduct surgery on White patients, searched for the right place to practice. They finally settled in Chicago, where Johnson studied music. She became an accomplished concert violinist and the first Black American to win a statewide violin competition. Then her father abandoned his family, leaving them in difficult financial and emotional circumstances.

Johnson soldiered on, mopping floors at JCPenney to help her family with groceries and expenses, even as she continued high school, graduated, and went to college. At the University of Illinois, she met Robert Johnson, who became her husband and business partner until their divorce in 2002. In the early years of their marriage, Sheila Johnson worked as a music teacher and founded a youth orchestra, but she always had an orientation toward risk-taking and entrepreneurial ventures. Robert Johnson was of the same bent. A television lobbyist, he realized an enormous change was coming to the industry with the arrival of satellite television and its national scope. Like the founders of ESPN, the Johnsons got in on the ground floor of the cable TV revolution, getting seed money to launch their own channel.

The difference was, instead of meeting the underserved needs of sports fanatics, the Johnsons recognized the underserved needs of Black consumers and businesses. To that point, television was overwhelmingly White in content, audience, and advertisement. BET (Black Entertainment Television) was the first network created for Black people, with Black sports, movies, TV shows, news, and, most notably, music videos. Black advertisers flocked to the channel, and the value of the business soared.

The Johnsons sold BET to Viacom in 2001. The equity they'd shared with early employees created multiple new millionaires. As Robert Johnson said, "That allowed the people that worked with me to share in the ownership, so when the company went public, they were given shares, and when the company was sold those shares turned into Viacom stock. To me, that's what you do as a founder; you bring your people in and give them a significant piece of the commitment to opportunity so that they feel that you commit to their success as much as you have to your own success."[8] In the process, the Johnsons themselves became billionaires.

Their marriage was not as successful, and Sheila Johnson left her husband after years of looking the other way with his affairs. She was now the nation's first Black female billionaire. Her new hometown of Middleburg, Virginia, was overwhelmingly White and wealthy. Johnson didn't like the confederate flag hanging from a local gun shop, so she bought the building and opened her own café and market called Market Salamander. The brand and the luxury concept intrigued her. So she bought more land over local resistance and founded a luxury hospitality business that would grow to seven hotels and resorts and become known as the Salamander Collection. She invested some of those windfalls in her hometown, supporting a private school and local civic infrastructure. At the suggestion of Sundance founder Robert Redford, she even founded a film festival in the town.

Sheila Johnson keeps expanding her empire. Today she also has ownership stakes in three Washington, DC–based teams, the Wizards, the Mystics, and the Capitals, becoming the first female owner of three franchises. She did so not just because of her keen understanding of sports and entertainment, but because sports ownership gives people a different kind of seat at the table of local politics, business, and society. She bought a golf resort in Florida for similar reasons. Sheila Johnson also became an executive producer of *A Powerful Noise*, a film about women leading struggles against ignorance, poverty, oppression, and ethnic conflict, and *Kicking It*, a documentary about soccer and its role in helping homeless people overcome addiction. She went on to launch nine soccer teams for homeless women.

Her independence, wealth, leadership, social status, and philanthropic impact were possible because Sheila Johnson chose the path of ownership.

EMPOWERING EACH UNIQUE LENS

One of the fundamental principles of investing is the importance of identifying overlooked or undervalued market opportunities. For this reason, it's puzzling why many venture capital firms do not fully appreciate the value of diversity in helping spot a variety of market needs. As we interviewed venture capital (VC) companies for this book, it became increasingly apparent that nontraditional sources of deal flow and entrepreneurial ideas rarely appeared on their radar screens. One firm appears to have programs to bring in diverse founders and board members. However, in the interview with their general partner, there was still a perception that the unique lens of diverse talent would take decades to impact their business.

In reality, general partners dedicating their funds to opportunities from diverse founders find significant and immediate deal flow.

And yet diverse founders, while they may face significant obstacles in access to capital, networks, and other resources, can have a distinct advantage in spotting overlooked or undervalued market opportunities. This is something that has been proven through research and startup work time and time again. Diverse founders can spot those needs because of their diverse backgrounds, experiences, perspectives, and networks. Ironically, even when those needs are brought to the attention of mainstream investors, they may still be undervalued because of the belief that those opportunities are not scalable across a large or broad enough range of consumers.

They're wrong.

Capitalizing on Innovation

We have encountered many innovators who spotted overlooked or undervalued problems, market needs, or business opportunities in their communities because of their diverse backgrounds, perspectives, and lived experiences. We spoke extensively with individuals who started companies because no other company, product, or service existed to serve their community or market needs. Additionally, some have launched their businesses in regions of the country where rent and talent are less expensive because other companies steer clear of those areas or ignore their undervalued resources. Ironically, those same innovators struggle to find the network and capital necessary to get their new businesses off the ground because they are not part of the mainstream.

The key to lasting or generational wealth, however, is ownership. Such wealth can be used to spawn more businesses, create more social impact, and grow more wealth in turn. But without ownership, the innovator can't fully capitalize on the value of their innovations.

Consider one of America's greatest and most prolific inventors as a historical example. Until he was 10 his name was Carver's George, after the man who owned him as an enslaved person from the day he was born. He flipped the name to George Carver and later added the W. to distinguish himself from a namesake in town. That W. never officially stood for Washington, but when someone suggested it might, Carver went along with it and became the George Washington Carver we know today from the history books, parks, streets, and monuments.[1]

Carver's father passed away shortly before he was born, and his mother and sister were kidnapped by slave raiders when he was just a week old. But his slave owner adopted him after abolition and raised him as part of his own family. Carver was a talented and intelligent boy who had a particular affinity for growing produce. He understood instinctively how to nurture plants and even develop new strains. His adoptive parents saw his acumen in this and other areas and gave Carver access to education. As he progressed through grades, he was forced to travel far to attend schools that allowed Blacks. Nevertheless, at each stop, his intelligence caught the attention of his teachers and propelled him farther along.

After high school, he was accepted into college in Kansas, but when he arrived, the administration refused to admit him because of the color of his skin. He turned to hired work as a farmer and ranch hand to get by, going back to his first love, growing plants and raising animals. A few years later, he tried to go back to school and secured a federal loan to support his education. This time, he chose to study art and piano, which were two of his other talents. His art teacher noticed his skill in painting flowers and plants, and convinced him to study botany instead. He went to Iowa State, where he was the university's first Black student. While there, he wrote his thesis on plant modification and began experimental research that was at the forefront of modern agriculture. Along the way, he became a teaching member of the faculty—again, the first Black person to have such a role at his institution.

Booker T. Washington, then head of the Tuskegee Institute, recruited Carver to become the head of the agriculture department. Over the next five decades, Carver continued work on his research, ultimately becoming one of the preeminent agricultural experts and scientists in the world. That research benefitted millions, including the families of former slave owners and the descendants of their enslaved laborers. The rich farming soil of the Black Belt had become depleted through its singular reliance on cotton. Carver's innovations helped restore soil health through crop rotation and applied nutrients, and ushered in a new era of verdancy. His research laboratory also developed and produced hundreds of new applications of crops that improved yields and food nutrition levels.

He became a public and political figure, lecturing widely on crop research, agricultural practices, and environmentalism, testifying at congressional hearings, consulting with presidents, and befriending industrialists, including Henry Ford. When he died, he bequeathed a sizable amount of money to create a foundation at the Tuskegee Institute. He had saved it by living frugally, not by capitalizing on his many breakthroughs and patentable inventions. Maybe he was not, at heart, a commercially minded person, but unlike many other innovators, from his friend Henry Ford to Thomas Edison and modern examples like Marc Andreessen and Elon Musk, he never gained the kind of wealth that might have changed the world. Some innovators have one or two great ideas available to them and turn those into capital that can be used to foster more innovation. A rare few have many ideas. Some like Carver and Edison have countless. But, while Carver's scientific work had a lasting impact on the lives of millions, there are no General Electrics, Ford Motor Companies, or Teslas to continue his legacy.

That's a loss to us all.

A Growing Need

Ashlie Thomas came to work at Eshelman Innovation through major good fortune. Thomas was running a laboratory on campus, and Eshelman was searching for a new project manager. She was a backup candidate for the role, but when the lead candidate dropped out, Thomas was interviewed. Her interview hinted at what was later discovered as a truly extraordinary tale of commitment and passion. She was nicknamed Blossom by members of the Eshelman team, as over the next few years, she bloomed into an amazing author, researcher, and entrepreneur. Thomas personifies what is possible when we engage diverse communities in innovation and entrepreneurship.

Thomas's entrepreneurship journey also weaves themes of this book together, and illustrates the power of innovation to transform individual lives and whole communities. Just as important, Ashlie's story captures the winding path that many entrepreneurs and innovators take to arrive where they seem destined to be.

Like many of the people mentioned earlier, Thomas's family is from the South but moved north during the Great Migration. She was born in Detroit, Michigan, in a home that her father inherited from her grandmother, a woman who owned many houses in the area until her death from cancer when Thomas was only six months old. Then, when she was nine, Thomas's family moved to Atlanta, Georgia, to be closer to her mother's family, returning to the South as so many others have done.

Though not wealthy, Thomas's family was solidly middle to upper-middle class. Her father worked in law enforcement, and her mother had a prominent position working for the president of Spelman College, the historically Black women's liberal arts college. She felt secure and sheltered from overt racism, crime, or hardship while growing up. She excelled at every aspect of school, from academics and sports to extracurricular activities, and seemed destined for medicine. As a young girl, her family had called her Little Dr. Ashlie because she'd carried around her own doctor's bag, insisting that it contained real bandages and instruments. Her parents were eager to ensure she had ample opportunities to live up to her potential. In her junior year of high school, Thomas set her sights on attending Spelman. That dream came true when she received early acceptance. She began her academic career at Spelman filled with high hopes. Then her life took a sudden and unexpected turn.

Thomas's family became a complex web of difficulties and worries. Her father's health was one. Like many Black men, he'd developed type-2 diabetes and hypertension, and Thomas, who wasn't afraid of illness or disease, helped him navigate many of the health challenges that came with managing diabetes. Unfortunately, the eventual split of her parents altered everyone's financial circumstances drastically. Suddenly, Thomas had to work three part-time jobs to keep herself enrolled at Spelman, even as she struggled with her increasingly tumultuous family life.

Thomas's grandparents were also struggling with chronic illnesses. Her grandfather had been on dialysis for years to treat kidney disease, and he developed heart disease. Her grandmother was not in good health, either. Without someone to look after her grandparents, their health would likely worsen. They clearly needed a caretaker. Thomas had always shared a deep bond with her grandparents, and their well-being was deeply important to her, so she knew she had to step in. At the beginning of her junior year, Thomas decided to leave Spelman and move to Effingham, South Carolina, where her grandfather had grown up on a farm that had been in the family for generations. This move not only provided the care they needed, but also offered Thomas a secure and stable refuge amidst the chaos of her life.

Though it was a heartbreaking decision, Thomas recognizes it as a defining moment that forced her to think deeply about her sense of purpose and direction. Despite her care, her grandfather's condition continued to deteriorate, and he entered end-stage kidney failure and needed a transplant. In addition to acting as his caregiver, Thomas became his advocate, pushing the doctors, nurses, and hospital administrators for the care he needed. Through this long, drawn-out ordeal, she felt increasingly jaded toward the medical profession and the healthcare system in general. Chronic illness had a significant impact on people's lives, but the healthcare profession did not do enough to address the root causes of their disease or to promote health.

It dawned on her that one of their biggest challenges was getting access to nutritious food. Ironically, Effingham was a small town surrounded by rich farmland and famous for a number of national brands of canned vegetables, but the community lacked high-quality grocery stores. In fact, her grandparents' home had once been part of a large, thriving farm owned by her great-great-grandfather. Some of her ancestors had even worked the land as enslaved people. Over the decades, however, that farm had been sold off section by section. This was a familiar story for many Black families in the South. Holding onto farms had been almost impossible because of discriminatory banking and taxation policies. It made her furious to think of that loss and the impact it continued to have on generations of people in her community, including her own family. Like her grandparents and father, many people around her suffered from chronic illnesses such as diabetes and heart failure, their lives diminished and cut short by unhealthy environments and stress, as well as their lack of access to healthy food. Everywhere she looked, there were dialysis centers but few grocery stores. How had this irrational and horrible situation become accepted as normal?

As a child, she'd loved watching her grandfather garden and grow vegetables. When his own brothers and sisters moved out of the house to attend college, he stayed behind to farm, even though farm work was looked down on by many in the Black community because of its association with slavery. Seeing the vastness of underutilized agricultural land in Effingham perplexed Thomas. How can there be so much land yet so few food options? Working the soil moved her in a way she hadn't felt since her life had taken such a sharp turn. She wondered, now, whether she could do something about that.

Over the next couple of years, Thomas finished her degree at Francis Marion University. During this time, she met her future husband, and together they decided to move to North Carolina for their careers. Thomas continued her career in microbiology and immunology research. Eventually, they moved her grandparents to North Carolina, where her grandfather received a kidney transplant after several lifestyle changes made him a better candidate. With her grandfather's health stabilizing and her family together in North Carolina, Thomas felt a renewed sense of purpose and possibility.

She and her husband purchased their home and built a garden with the intention of increasing their nutritious food access for themselves and their family. She started sharing her passion for gardening on social media under the online persona "The Mocha Gardener." Her gardening lessons struck a chord with a growing number of social media followers around the world.

Ashlie continued to grow food and run her blog even while working full time. Eventually, she began taking graduate courses through the University of North Carolina system. This time, she didn't pursue medicine but nutrition. Instead of studying the world through a microscope, as she had in her lab, she began to look at it through a larger societal lens. She noticed the same food insecurity challenges in North Carolina that she'd seen in Effingham. There were plenty of fast-food restaurants but few quality grocery stores, and chronic illness was everywhere.

Some students are content to take their courses and do research; however, Thomas wanted to find answers to help her community. She reached out to advisors and mentors about nutrition, food access, and chronic illness, filled with a sense of mission. How do we begin to fix this? Food insecurity wasn't just a local challenge; it was a global issue that had a profound impact on the lives of countless people and communities.

As she immersed herself in health equity and food security-based community work while pursuing her academic research to explore the problem in depth, Ashlie became consumed with finding practical ways to make a difference. She didn't believe that she could accomplish much through healthcare or politics—they were too entrenched and big to move. But she became increasingly intrigued by the possibilities of business—particularly in how it's leveraged to help solve complex societal problems in a sustainable way. Around the same time, she joined Eshelman Innovation at the University of North Carolina.

Eshelman Innovation was unusual because it had been founded to catalyze innovation in disease treatments, drug delivery systems, and healthcare practices by combining academic research with entrepreneurs and entrepreneurial ventures. The goal of the institute was to think boldly, take risks, strive for real impact, build sustainable businesses, and generate wealth and capital that could perpetuate the cycle of innovation and impact through future generations.

Thomas felt inspired by the energy, activity, and sense of possibility all around her. She also felt seen, encouraged, and deeply supported. In addition to her training and experience, the team also valued Thomas's lived experiences, perspectives, and her Blackness, which was unique for an academic setting. They were as interested in the innovator as the innovation.

The team encouraged Thomas's passion for making change; in fact, the most common refrain she heard was "Think bigger." With that kind of support and modeling, Thomas began to think and act like an entrepreneur. She was tired of waiting for the world to recognize the importance of food security to overall health. Societal changes were happening, but not quickly enough. She realized she could push things along by strategically and deliberately promoting gardening. For many Black people, there was still a stigma associated with working the land, another toxic legacy of slavery, but to Thomas, "gardening gives people and communities the power to take back ownership over their own health and their capacity to thrive."[2] What could she do to promote that further? She had social media influence and a brand, but how could she turn that into a business that could be monetized to support her financially while she scaled her impact more deliberately and effectively?

The conversations, connections, and experiences at the institute were invaluable in that discovery process. She saw firsthand, over and over, how innovators turned their passion into businesses that met customer or market needs. She also got valuable feedback on her own business ideas. She managed to weave several of her activities more quickly than she thought possible. She turned her educational social media platform into a source of revenue, monetizing her brand. Very quickly, she received recognition for that through major magazines like *Better Homes and Gardens,* and she was eventually approached by a publisher to write a book, which helped generate more consulting work and paid speaking engagements around agriculture's role in improving food systems and nutrition security in communities.

Even as her vision comes to life, it continues to expand. Thomas is completing her master's in food and nutritional sciences while also working on a digital platform that can connect people and communities to resources, education, and technology solutions that promote healthier nutrition and encourage healthier behaviors. By thinking like an innovator, she's learning to leverage her assets for the betterment of others and to grow her own wealth and influence.

In recent months, Thomas has experienced an increasingly accelerated ride on her startup journey, bringing her company TerraLink to the next level. The concept behind TerraLink is to leverage technology to streamline the food production, access, and nutrition education pipeline for communities. She's been collaborating closely with organizations (including Nex Cubed and the HBCU Founders Initiative described in Chapter 7) that have introduced her to advisors who helped her think through her venture across multiple fronts, including business plan, technology, resources, and funding. In December 2023, she participated in a Demo Day with the goal of selling this software-as-a-service (SaaS) solution to health systems and other organizations increasingly concerned about nutrition access, the treatment of chronic illnesses, and solutions for addressing gaps in social determinants and health equity within their communities. At the end of her presentation, a potential backer from an academic medical center stood up and said that Thomas's innovation was exactly the kind of solution his organization was looking for. Since then, Thomas has had numerous in-depth conversations with other organizations about participating in pilots and programs to test and build out her solution and bring it to scale.

Thomas's story is emblematic of other stories in food, health and wellness, beauty, and sport that have a founder from a diverse background who takes their unique insights and addresses a business opportunity.

The Food Opportunity

Through her personal experience, interest, and aptitude, Thomas discovered a market need within her community for healthy food. She is not alone. Food and nutrition generally, and food as medicine specifically, have become highly attractive areas of interest for investors. In October 2022, for example, a group of investors calling themselves the Food, Nutrition, and Health Investor Coalition announced that they had pooled $2.5 billion to support opportunities with startups focusing on improving health through nutritious food and related technologies.[3]

Compton Vegan aims to combat the same food insecurity problems that Thomas is working to solve. The founder, Lemel Durrah, grew up in the south Los Angeles city of Compton, one of the oldest and most ethnically and historically rich cities in America. The city became a draw for middle-class Black families in the 1950s, particularly from the rural South, because of the availability of large houses and small plots of farmland. The Watts Uprising of 1965 tilted the city into a long economic decline, despite its suburban appeal, as many middle-class, and particularly White, families fled. By 1969, Compton had the highest crime rate in California. By the 1980s, Compton was a center of violent gang warfare between the Bloods and the Crips and a center for music innovation with the rise of West Coast gangster rap. One of those bands, NWA, spawned many incredibly influential musicians, including Dr. Dre, who also became a heralded music producer and entrepreneur, co-founding Beats Electronics, a music headphone and streaming company, which was sold to Apple in 2014 for $3.4 billion.

Growing up in Compton, Lemel Durrah witnessed firsthand the devastating impact of diabetes, hypertension, and chronic heart and kidney disease on his community. A city that once flourished because of its small farms and home-cooked meals had become a food desert. None of the quality grocers like Whole Foods would open stores in Compton, despite the market need, and people only had fast food to turn to. Durrah quit his job as a teacher to open Compton Vegan, a food service that produces and delivers plant-based food. Durrah focuses on producing vegan dishes that are close to traditional meals familiar to Black families. He also started his own community garden to grow the necessary produce and speaks widely on the importance of nutrition and physical and mental health. He knows there are food deserts in every urban center in America, and his vision is to open a Compton Vegan across from fast-food restaurants around the country.

Innovators in marginalized communities often have unique or particularly insightful perspectives on local market needs. Their innovations may directly target marginalized communities, but their even greater value is the scalability of those ideas to mainstream communities and broader markets. Through innovation, we all win. We win more when we empower innovators with unique or alternative perspectives to test their assumptions, develop their products or services, and profit and grow from their successful efforts.

A company called Gro Intelligence is a case in point. The founder, Sara Menker, grew up in Ethiopia in a middle-class family but witnessed the impact of climate-related famine on her country. After attending college in the United States and Britain, she became an analyst at Morgan Stanley but continued to think about the possibilities of data analytics to predict the impact of climate change and food shortages. She started Gro Intelligence as a data analytics platform that absorbs immense quantities of data from a broad range of sources to make agricultural commodity forecasts. Gro Intelligence's artificial intelligence engine can monitor and predict demand, supply, and prices for food around the world while giving farmers, policymakers, insurers, and businesses insights to navigate and predict climate risk and mitigate the impact of food shortages, adverse climate events, disease, economic swings, and workforce changes.

Out of her particular experience, education, and skillset, Menker has developed a fast-growing company that helps us all.

The Health and Wellness Opportunity

US healthcare is one of the most active sectors for startups and investors, with good reason. Healthcare is a $3 trillion industry that consumes almost 20 percent of GDP. Investment in healthcare digital technology startups peaked in 2021 at almost $30 billion, and returned to Earth in 2022 at nearly $13 billion, but the sector continues to be rife with innovation and activity.[4]

Chapter 6 more closely examines the growing amount of capital being invested in Black- and minority-founded startups. Those investments are recognition of enormous market needs in many sectors, but perhaps especially healthcare.

Compared to White people, Black people have significantly higher incidences of illness, cancer death, and infant mortality. Black people have less access to care, face more discrimination in gaining access, and disproportionately lack coverage in states that do not participate in Medicaid expansion under the Affordable Care Act. Black people are far more likely than White people to face social barriers to health, such as food insecurity, housing insecurity, and poverty.[5] Awareness of these disparities has grown since COVID because of the heightened impact of the disease on minorities and marginalized communities. However, innovators from Black and minority communities are increasingly gaining traction in addressing market challenges around health equity, access, and other factors that impede health. In doing so, they're benefitting all.

Dasia Taylor was a 17-year-old high school student in Iowa City when she developed sutures that change color when they detect infection. Taylor had learned about smart sutures coated with a conductive material that senses infection by monitoring changes in electrical resistance around a wound. These smart sutures then relay that information digitally to inform doctors and patients. She immediately realized that lack of access to smartphones or computers would be a significant barrier to benefitting from such innovation. This was particularly the case in the developing world, where 11 percent of surgical wounds develop infection. In some African countries, for example, up to 20 percent of women who give birth by C-section later develop infections in their surgical wounds.[6]

Taylor thought of a different way to use sutures as an indicator of infection. She knew that human skin is naturally acidic, but its pH level soars when a wound becomes infected. She also knew that many fruits and vegetables, such as beets, change color when their pH levels change. In her experiments, Taylor discovered that a cotton-polyester thread dyed with beet juice changes from bright red to dark purple in the presence of infection.

While aimed at a health challenge in developing countries, Taylor's invention can also specifically benefit Black women in America, who are more likely to die of infection after C-sections than White women. At the same time, all can benefit. The US suture market is projected to grow from $3.41 billion in 2021 to $5.12 billion by 2028.[7]

As a health economist and father, Thompson Aderinkomi experienced a lot of frustration with the healthcare business model. After a particularly unpleasant and expensive visit to a primary care clinic with his one-year-old son in 2011, he launched Minneapolis-based Retrace Health, a company built to deliver quality primary care at the lowest cost and highest convenience possible. Retrace relied on nurse practitioners to diagnose, take care of lab work, and prescribe medications virtually or at the patient's home. Instead of paying for those visits with insurance, Retrace's customers paid a monthly fee for unlimited access. This effectively made Retrace a value-based care company, at full risk for its customers' health.

Aderinkomi was able to raise enough money to bring the business to scale, but had a disagreement over strategic direction with his largest investor. That investor forced Aderinkomi out of the company and installed their own CEO. Within a year, Retrace ceased business operations, unable to succeed in what it called a crowded primary care market.[8] Aderinkomi didn't share that view. Six months after his ouster, he started a new company, Nice Healthcare, that replicated the Retrace business model, with many of the same employees and customers; the business proceeded to flourish and grow.

Nice Healthcare has grown 300 percent every year since, with 10 times the revenue achieved by Retrace when it was shut down. Nice focuses on employers who pay for convenient, unlimited access to healthcare services for their employees at a fixed monthly fee. Since launch, Nice has raised $42 million in funds and established operations in 12 states with over 400 business company customers.

By providing unlimited services, Nice Healthcare prevents more acute and costly health conditions. During COVID-19, when many primary care practices struggled, Nice thrived because of its membership model. Aderinkomi intends to expand the model across the United States, focusing primarily on cities typically overlooked by venture-backed healthcare companies.

Ellington West is the co-founder and CEO of Sonavi Labs, a Baltimore-based medical device and software company. She came into technology naturally, as her father, James West, is the renowned inventor of the foil electric microphone, a technology used in almost all microphones today. James West developed the microphone technology when he worked at Bell Labs, and today, he holds over 60 patents and teaches at Johns Hopkins University, where he also supports programs and opportunities for minorities in science and business. Remarkably, his grandmother had been an enslaved person, but his mother had found work at NASA as one of the four African American "hidden figures," women who solved complex computational problems that helped advance the space program in the early sixties.

Sonavi emerged from Johns Hopkins research with Feelix, a smart stethoscope and AI-enabled platform that uses machine learning to detect and monitor respiratory problems remotely. Ellington West has helped Sonavi transition from a research project to a successful health tech company that has raised over $6.5 million and been awarded nine patents. She is one of fewer than 100 Black women who have raised over $1 million for her company. She believes strongly in the power of diversity and diverse perspectives in developing solutions that meet real needs:

> *Whether a company is developing a new drug, technology, software, or process, they should consider the full range of users. We've seen this happen in everything from the development of therapeutics that lacked diversity in clinical trials to automated sensors that can't detect dark skin. If companies aren't intentional about seeking diverse leadership and perspectives, then it will show in their products, marketing, and the faces, words, and actions of their team.*[9]

Certainly, as with Nice Healthcare and Sonavi Labs, the healthcare industry has also benefitted from Incredible Health, a platform for matching full-time nurses with open positions at hospitals. It was co-founded by Iman Abuzeid, who was born in Saudi Arabia to Sudanese parents. With the immense need for nursing in American healthcare, Incredible Health has seen tremendous growth. Over 10,000 nurses join the service each month, and the company now employs 180 people when the business secured $80 million in new funding in August 2022, which put its valuation into unicorn status, making Abuzeid one of only a few Black women ever to run a company valued at over $1 billion.[10]

The Sports and Entertainment Opportunity

Sports and entertainment is another sector of the economy experiencing tremendous growth and transformation because of digital technology.

Tyrre Burks took his experience as an athlete and turned it into Players Health, a platform for coach credentialing, injury reports, team management, and abuse investigations. Burks grew up on Chicago's South Side with his mother and says that sports saved his life. He attended college on a football scholarship and played in the Canadian Football League, but injuries derailed his career. When his career as a pro ball player ended, he started a sports communication app. But soon after, considering his own history of injuries, he sought ways to improve the experience of sports for young people.

Players Health, now based in Minneapolis, tracks injuries and diagnoses for young athletes, ensuring they don't return to their sport until it is safe for them to do so. It enables sports organizations—including leagues and teams—to manage compliance and insurance. It also sells insurance as a brokerage, topping $40 million in policy sales in 2022. In March 2022, Players Health raised $28 million in venture capital funding to fuel its expansion and growth.[11]

Harold Hughes is the founder and CEO of Greenville, South Carolina-based Bandwagon, an analytics and experience company that helps teams and entertainers create personalized fan experiences and eliminate ticket fraud. Hughes was born in New York but grew up in Jamaica and has a strong cultural love of community building. Bandwagon relies on data and blockchain technology to enable fans and consumers to be content creators, forming and showcasing memories and experiences that connect them to their favorite entertainers and brands while building community among like-minded followers. He found inspiration in how individuals from different backgrounds, religions, races, socioeconomic classes, and regions could unite over a cultural event like a football game.[12] It was about hugging and high-fiving when celebrating a team win. In this way, technology was bringing people together through shared experience, rather than dividing them.

Hughes was an exceptional student, earning two degrees in four years at Clemson University. He expected to attend law school but began working at a technology company after graduation, moving from inside sales to managing massive accounts over the next eight years while earning his MBA at Clemson and a graduate certificate in Innovation and

Entrepreneurship at Stanford University. After being headhunted for a CEO position at another tech firm, Hughes moved to Austin, Texas, where he and his wife started a family. Six months later, the position ended, and Hughes was left with a young family and two mortgages.

For many, it might have been time to scramble and find new employment. But Hughes saw a different opportunity. He'd been working on a startup idea for some years, thinking about the market, the ancillary products, and the technology. Now seemed like as good a time as any to give it the attention and resources it required. He sold one of his homes and started bootstrapping in 2016. After proving the concept and beginning to generate revenue, he raised $3 million in venture capital.

Hughes was drawn to entrepreneurship for the opportunities he saw in the market, but also for the calling he felt to make a difference for his community and for fellow creatives, technologists, and entrepreneurs of color. He didn't see many colleagues who looked like him. He didn't see his beliefs and values recognized or represented in society or corporate America. At a time when awareness of police violence against Black people was growing, Hughes could have stayed safe in a corporate job but he was driven to try to change unfounded and biased perceptions that Black people can't be successful business leaders, startup founders, technology experts, and wealth-generators.

Whenever Hughes discusses his professional journey, he makes sure to mention that he is a founder without a Harvard or Stanford pedigree or an alumnus status from Google or Facebook. He built his company in South Carolina, thousands of miles away from Silicon Valley. He views these as strikes against him—especially because he understands the playbook for venture capital is mostly written by White men.

With Bandwagon, Hughes plans to build a special company that amplifies community, even as he disrupts mainstream perceptions and expectations, and demonstrates new paths to success, wealth, and impact for people like him. In line with that, he mentors other entrepreneurs and has made angel investments in over 30 minority-founded companies.

The Beauty Opportunity

The $49 billion US cosmetic industry has long been controlled by a small handful of global companies.[13] Not surprisingly, those companies have paid little attention to the beauty and wellness needs of minorities and marginalized communities.

Like Madam C. J. Walker in the early 1900s, Ciara Imani May saw an opportunity to provide Black women with better, healthier beauty products. Most hair extensions are made from plastic, which can cause scalp irritation and even cancer. Such plastic is also energy-intensive to make and hard to recycle. She estimates that 30 million pounds of synthetic hair are disposed of each year in the United States. May wondered why there weren't more sustainable options available for Black hair care. She founded Rebundle in 2019 to offer biodegradable hair extensions made from banana fibers and recycled braiding hair. Rebundle raised $1.4 million in early-stage funding in January 2022.[14]

Robyn Rihanna Fenty was born in Barbados, and brought her Caribbean-influenced music to America, becoming the second-highest-selling female recording artist of all time. She's also America's youngest female self-made billionaire, not because of her music but her fashion brand, Fenty.

In 2017, Rihanna launched her cosmetics company, Fenty Beauty, as a brand within Paris-based LVMH, the global conglomerate specializing in luxury goods, including Louis Vuitton. Rihanna was inspired to start Fenty Beauty because of her lifelong love of make-up and the void she saw in the cosmetics industry for products that work with a variety of skin tones and types. Her success demonstrates the immense untapped value in meeting the needs of underserved or overlooked markets.

The company was founded with an ethic that its beauty products should exclude no one. "Beauty for All" was the marketing mission. It started with 40 different shades of foundation to encompass the full range of skin tones. The success of the business also lies in its distribution. The brand went live in 17 countries at once, requiring a complex array of supply chains, marketers, social media teams, and retailers to work in concert.[15] Sales immediately exceeded expectations, fueled by delighted customers taking selfies around the world.

More importantly, Fenty Beauty disrupted the traditional cosmetics industry and helped move it toward inclusivity and diversity. Other brands were forced to follow suit, not only because of Fenty's social leadership but also because of its incredible market success. Customers now demanded something they previously hadn't realized could be made.

# 6

ACCELERATING TRANSFORMATIVE CHANGE BY SUPPORTING INNOVATION

The extraordinary events of May 2020, when George Floyd was killed by police officer Derek Chauvin in Minneapolis, marked an important period during the early writing stages of this book. A wave of protests followed, propelled by an outflow of disgust at the blatant violence. A range of voices—some household names and others known within their respective spaces—emerged during this time. One voice that stood out was Marcus Whitney, who challenged his friends in Nashville to step up to the plate and drive change. Whitney had a unique story to tell. Despite a relatively privileged beginning, he had his own early struggles in life but had come to represent an example of a successful Black entrepreneur. His support on Black-led ventures is, in particular, a remarkable example of the opportunities that can be discovered when actively sought.

In June 2020, two weeks after the murder of George Floyd in Minneapolis, Whitney published an open letter to Nashville's healthcare leaders. As co-founder of Jumpstart Foundry, a fund for early-stage healthcare startups, he wrote the letter because the Nashville Health Care Leadership Council had not said a word in support of Black Lives Matter, nor made any acknowledgment of the impact of systemic racism on the city's healthcare ecosystem. As a Black man, Whitney's anger over George Floyd's death and the larger problems of racism got channeled into a powerful invitation to join him in making change happen.

The intended audience of healthcare leaders knew Whitney well. He was a member of the prestigious Nashville Health Care Fellows; a partner to Jumpstart's limited partnerships (LPs) among the region's thriving healthcare business community; a convener of the city's largest ever healthcare conference; a compelling voice for innovation, entrepreneurialism, social justice, and health equity; and a personal friend to many elite and influential White healthcare leaders. But now he spelled out explicitly why their inaction had triggered his response.

He noted that the healthcare industry had created $46.7 billion in economic impact for the region in 2018, more than any other sector, and that several of the city's healthcare businesses had become national giants, producing multiple White billionaires and many millionaires. He explained that the city's healthcare industry had its roots in White supremacy, and how it continued to fail its Black population in very real terms today, noting that, compared to their White neighbors, Nashville's Blacks have diminished health status and lifespans.[1] He then asked:

> *If Nashville's healthcare industry isn't suffering from systemic racism, tell me then:*
>
> *How is it possible that the nation's leading healthcare services cluster has generated incredible wealth for White people in Nashville but no meaningful wealth for Nashville's Black community?*
>
> *How is it possible that in a city where Black people make up twenty-seven percent of the population, the board of the Nashville Health Care Council representing the industry leaders has one Black person at the table out of thirty filled seats?*
>
> *How is it that Nashville is home to Meharry Medical College, one of the top five producers of Black primary care physicians in the US, and Tennessee State University which has a public health, health administration, and health sciences bachelor's programs, yet there is no formal pipeline from those institutions into significant leadership positions within the industry-leading companies that Nashville is home to?*[2]

Whitney went on to speak uncomfortable truths about his success as a Black man founding a startup in the city. Without a White male partner, he would never have had access to venture capital in the city; without White men in positions of power sharing power with him, he never would have gotten the support and connections he needed to succeed. And without that power, those connections, and that capital, he would not have felt free to speak his mind. He was one of only a few Black people in the city who had the status and independence to do so.

To remedy that, he called on Nashville's healthcare leaders to "start doing real work in diversifying leadership to reflect the employees and communities they serve. You can't have a company full of Black people at the bottom with only White people at the top and not acknowledge the systemic racism in that."[3] He acknowledged it would take time, and that the path forward was not clear and would need to be collaboratively developed, but the moment to start was now.

A Moment of Need, a Time for Change?

There was nothing straightforward or inevitable about the path that Whitney took in bringing him to the point where he could write such a letter and have it read, acknowledged, and acted upon. He was born in New York City to parents who were in their forties when they had him. Committed to his education, they enrolled Whitney in an elite public school for gifted and talented children. Then, they saved to send him to prep school with smaller class sizes rather than enroll him in one of the neighborhood schools, which they saw as overcrowded and unruly. Whitney soaked up his gifted and talented education and crammed his day with school athletics, starting early, and finishing late. He also immersed himself in computers. His uncle worked at IBM upstate and gave him an IBM PC Junior for Christmas one year, back when personal computers needed to be programmed to do anything. So, Whitney learned basic programming even as the internet was starting to become an area of intense interest for nerds in computer labs.

The one thing he didn't learn was self-management. He'd relied far more than he realized on his highly structured and very full schedule to keep himself on track and successful. College life, at the young age of 17, was more than he could handle. Drawn to hip-hop music, he dropped out after two years and headed to Atlanta to start a record label. There, he and his wife had a child together, and he woke up to the reality that he was a college dropout with job in music that wasn't going to support them.

ACCELERATING TRANSFORMATIVE CHANGE BY SUPPORTING INNOVATION

He started to hustle, doing whatever he could to make money, bill collecting, waiting tables. He and his wife decided to leave Atlanta for Nashville, her hometown, so they could tap into more support. On Labor Day 2000, they packed up the car and headed west. Nashville was only a little easier; Whitney still needed to make money waiting tables while they lived in a hotel room they rented by the week. But their desperate circumstances sparked more determination. Whitney turned back to computers and taught himself how to code. The internet was the hottest thing going on in the economy. He got a job the day after his second son was born, working as a junior programmer for a company called Health Stream, which ended up being one of the last internet startups to go public before the bubble burst.

Though the crash was tough, he was now on a better path and spent the next seven years as a professional programmer. Two years later, he got a job at an email marketing firm, which quickly recognized his talent and hired him full time as employee number five. With some financial security at last, he lifted his head from his coding work and began to study other aspects of business. Technology was just one slice of a successful company. There were also sales, marketing, customer service, finance, and strategy. Intensely curious about it all, Whitney tried to learn everything he could. How to create software, how to build a team, how to run a business. The company grew fast, and soon there were 50 employees and $15 million in revenue. Whitney was offered a job by another company, but he didn't want to leave his current position. Instead, he asked for a raise and a share in the company's equity. It wasn't his first instinct to be so bold, but he was learning to advocate for his value. He was grateful when management agreed to his request, knowing that it was a fair reflection of his worth to the company.

The equity stake was a meaningful event in Whitney's life. Eventually, he did end up leaving the company, using the proceeds from selling his equity back to them as capital to jumpstart his entrepreneurial endeavors. The year 2007 was pivotal. The iPhone was launched, and social media, mobile computing, and what would become the cloud started to gain steam. Whitney went to South by Southwest and connected with a larger network of startup and digital tech leaders. He transitioned from being a programmer to a technology entrepreneur and began his education in the venture capital space. He also started working nights and weekends to launch a tech accelerator called Jumpstart Our Country with his new business partner, Vic Gatto.

The accelerator showed real promise. Whitney and Vic decided to commit full time and pivoted to a healthcare-only startup fund they called Jumpstart Foundry. Suddenly, Whitney was making things happen everywhere he turned. He even brought a professional soccer team to Nashville as a minority owner. But most of his attention was on healthcare startups, finding them, assessing them, deciding whether to invest in them, and connecting entrepreneurs to leading healthcare organizations in Nashville where they could gain traction for their services and platforms.

Then came 2020. COVID. George Floyd. A racial reckoning across America. And the letter to the Nashville Health Care Leadership Council. Whitney called for meaningful change to right historic wrongs in the Nashville healthcare sector. Across the country, the national healthcare conversation had suddenly turned to health equity. Rather than focus on patient or health issues, Whitney honed in on disparities in board makeup, executive team diversity, and capital allocation because those were the levers that ultimately drove disparities in health outcomes.

After a lifetime of being the only Black person in every room, Whitney had the credibility and the economic freedom to make a point when that moment came, and he felt an immense responsibility to write that letter.

He didn't know what to expect, but the letter generated serious conversations among the Council about how they deployed capital and how they fostered entrepreneurship. That momentum inspired Whitney to launch Jumpstart Nova, a fund for Black-led healthcare startups. Within three months of publishing his letter, Whitney started raising funds for his new fund. He closed a first round in December 2020, and a final round a year later. He started investing that capital in January 2021.

Two years in, Marcus had a $55 million seed and a Series A healthcare venture fund and made nine investments with a fairly simple investment model. The companies they invested in focused on the United States and were Black-founded. Other details reflected their preferences and experience: markets they think are working, companies they think are exciting, and founders they believed in.

Contrary to the expectations of some prominent observers, there was no shortage of promising Black-led healthcare startups to invest in. When he wrote his letter, Whitney had no data to back his claims, but his thesis has proven out. The fund turned down 200 companies and is actively engaging with around 120 of them until they're ready for seed. And the entrepreneurs they did turn down knew the rejection wasn't because of their race; it was because of fit, readiness, or some other factor.

Whitney believes that Black founders need support beyond funding; they need exposure, access, and partners ready to help them succeed. However, Whitney's vision for Jumpstart Nova was even bigger. Its long-term goal is to create a net-new institution that can be a center of Black healthcare innovation in the United States.

Whitney is making that happen. Fortunately, he's no longer the only Black person in the room. Others are also working toward a similar goal because they see the tremendous untapped opportunity for returns.

Models of Innovation Acceleration

The startup support world is murky and mysterious. Various approaches, models, and philosophies have been created to serve founders, surface good ideas, accelerate success, and unleash wealth creation. Some are largely funding focused; others provide work, space, and time; some aim to incubate or accelerate startups through facilitated introductions, connections to sponsors, and developmental training; others combine all of the above. Which approaches are most effective? What problems do they solve? How well do they resolve gaps? How aligned are they with the real needs of founders and the best market-based solutions? Most importantly, how do they identify who should get the funding, space, and support they provide?

In theory, startups are selected based on their potential for growth and return on investment. To that end, they are given help to achieve what they cannot manage as easily or quickly otherwise. The idea that such investment or support is morally neutral and blind to race, gender, age, ethnicity, language, education, and more is provably and obviously false.

Venture capital investors, for example, are 90 percent male and 72 percent White. In 2020, only 2.6 percent of VC funding went to minority founders overall, 2.2 percent to women founders,[4] and 1 percent to Black founders.[5] Minority and female founders face numerous barriers to funding, and can benefit massively from capital, development, training, and access to customers.

Not only are minority and women founders often overlooked as investment targets, but the value or worth of their solutions is often overlooked as well. Funders, gatekeepers, mentors, sponsors, and so on may be unaware of the potential demand for a solution in markets they don't personally understand or haven't directly experienced. In this sense, those investors and supporters may be acting contrary to their own best interests. After all, the most lucrative investments can be the ones that others (at least initially) overlook or undervalue. Few ideas, founders, or startups succeed wildly. But it can be very profitable to support a founder with the germ of an idea or an early-stage company that ends up making a dent in the markets. Indeed, most venture funds rely on those rare hits to support their total portfolio of investments.

This is where Eshelman Innovation Institute comes into the picture. Co-author John Bamforth came to the institute bringing his corporate experience and passion for leveraging all innovators in its mandate. The question was how. Bamforth and the institute's leaders studied the data and consulted numerous experts in the space, including innovators, entrepreneurs, and investors, to gain insights from their lived experiences and perspectives. They developed the germ of a thesis, then engaged the team at the institute to gain their commitment and dedication to the goal of supporting minority founders. This mission was whole-heartedly embraced and became a core underpinning of the institute's work. Through serendipity, the institute already had a diverse team representing a broad array of backgrounds and cultural experiences; nonetheless, the dialogue on the subject of race, entrepreneurship, and social gaps was rich and filled with challenging discussions. These discussions frequently introduced new ideas and viewpoints. Even Bamforth, who had initiated the work, was often challenged on his approach, especially when his unconscious biases showed up in decisions. With the team and culture established, the final step was to determine how to best make a dent in the broader societal issues at hand.

The team began its journey by collaborating with a fellow university in the UNC system, North Carolina A&T, the largest historically Black university in the country. The institute formed a partnership with A&T that would pair them and Chapel Hill faculty to generate novel ideas for the institute to fund for development. However, after two years of trying, this initiative failed miserably to deliver a single collaborative project that would work. The institute's team was surprised, frustrated, and deeply disappointed. Both parties genuinely wanted to collaborate, so what was the problem? After months of debate and dialogue, it was determined that the failure was due to a combination of factors. First, the faculty and research enterprise at A&T were significantly underfunded relative to UNC-Chapel Hill and its $1.2 billion-a-year budget. Second, A&T faculty had a significant teaching load and minimal time and resources for research. Lastly, the institute lacked an innovation model to support the ideas from A&T. Given the challenging circumstances before them, the institute felt an urgent need to rethink how it would engage with their HBCU colleagues.

Fortunately, the institute had begun to develop a rich vein of innovative exploration in digital health, leveraging the outstanding health sciences schools on campus. Members of the team had become fans of an emerging asset class in venture funding called the venture studio. They asked themselves, "Could this model be applied within our partnership at A&T?" Impatient for wins and wondering if this could be the path forward, they did a rapid run of due diligence and identified Nex Cubed and the HBCU Founders Fund as potential partners.

The HBCU Founders Fund was launched in February 2023 by Marlon Evans, CEO of Nex Cubed, an investment fund and incubator for digital health and fintech companies. The Founders Fund is a $40 million venture studio and pre-seed fund that focuses on startups where at least one founder is an HBCU student, alum, or faculty member.

Evans has an interesting story of how he came to see the value and the imperative of supporting entrepreneurs connected to HBCUs. He was born in Maryland to parents from Trinidad. When his father, who worked for the International Development Bank, was assigned to Jamaica, the family moved with him. They moved back to Maryland a few years later. Along the way, Evans was exposed to the impact that finance could have on the world through development projects.

An excellent football player, Evans got the opportunity to play and study at Stanford University. He likely wouldn't have thought to follow that path if his sister hadn't attended Stanford before him. It was a decision that changed his life. As a center of innovation and entrepreneurialism, Stanford was an exciting place for a young person who wanted to make an impact on the world. Evans got a firsthand education in the power of innovation to shape companies, markets, and communities.

After graduation, he looked for a way to make his own impact on the world and focused on education. For his first job, he ended up working at Stanford's admissions office, visiting schools all over the country as a recruiter. He loved the experience but knew most of the students he met attended elite schools, had affluent upbringings, and had access to all the resources in the world when countless more students couldn't compete for such opportunities. That's when he decided to shift his focus to helping students who would otherwise be underrepresented in elite environments like Stanford.

To that end, he went to work for an organization called the Knowledge Is Power Program (KIPP), a foundation that launched high-performing charter schools in low-income communities. His role was to identify areas without good public school options, establish a charter program, and recruit students by going door-to-door and talking to parents. He enjoyed the work, but even though the schools were successful, in the end, the impact felt like a drop in the bucket. He was helping a few thousand students, but there were millions more in the public school system without access to the opportunities of a great education.

Seeking a bigger platform, he went to work running the Ronnie Lott Foundation called All Stars Helping Kids, which supported KIPP and other organizations like Citizen Schools and Junior Achievement. He felt his breadth of impact growing. Then he was recruited by HP as its director of corporate affairs. His primary interest in taking the role was to lead company-wide foundation programs such as Matter to a Million, which empowered employees to make microloans in developing nations. Evans was excited to have access to 300,000 employees in 170 countries, along with nearly unlimited resources, talent, and technology. However, he soon realized that the bureaucracy of a large organization was an immense barrier to progress and urgency. While the potential impact was huge, it took months to get approval for even the smallest decisions.

After leaving HP, he landed at GSVlabs as CEO, an organization focused on accelerating startups and connecting them to corporate sponsors. Evans was following on the heels of other famous accelerators, including Techstars and Y Combinator, but the focus was on real estate with some innovation on the side. That wasn't enough for Evans, so when Nex Cubed called and asked him to help launch their startup accelerator, he was intrigued. He warned the board that part of his mission would be to figure out how to create more social impact through the fund. They embraced his vision and waited for his direction.

His efforts at social impact started by ensuring the fund's portfolio represented the real world in ways that typical startup funds failed to do. Evans wanted to create an environment where all founders from all backgrounds felt welcomed. There were more than enough exceptional minority- and women-led initiatives to invest in. Within five years, the fund built a portfolio of over 80 investments, 60 percent of which were led by either entrepreneurs of color or women. Today, the Nex Cubed portfolio holds over 70 companies with an aggregate value of $450 million.

After George Floyd's murder, Nex Cubed, like many organizations, looked around to see what more it could do to rectify inequities and increase social impact. Sure, compared to their peers, the fund was crushing it with its investments in minority founders, but a dilemma persisted.

They were only drawing from founders who had already raised capital from angel investors, friends and family, or institutional investors. Considering the enormous swathe of people without access to such resources, they decided to explore ways to widen their funnel.

With his experience at Stanford, Evans understood how rich and vibrant a campus environment could be, and he wondered about untapped potential at historically Black colleges and universities (HBCUs) around the country. After a little research, Evans and his team realized there weren't really any other accelerators or funds out there trying to tap entrepreneurs and founders at HBCUs. Sometimes a corporation would parachute in to do a hackathon or engage in some other one-off event, but they were soon gone, and sustainable, long-term efforts to cultivate founders and create connections were lacking.

After making some overtures to a couple of HBCUs, Nex Cubed was inundated with interest and realized the opportunity was immense. At the time, it was also very easy to get corporate interest in supporting their efforts. Everyone they approached raised their hand to help. They decided to give their thesis a try by testing the waters with an accelerator program.

The number and quality of applications was overwhelming. Not every idea was likely to become the next Microsoft, but most showed promise and a keen understanding of underserved market needs. Evans and the team designed the application process to make sure that interested founders got value whether they were able to participate in the program or not. The team gave them feedback they might not otherwise have been able to receive. In the summer of 2021, Nex Cubed selected nine teams and hosted their first HBCU-focused accelerator. It awarded each team $10,000 in non-dilutive funding, basically a grant for each team, and invited them to San Francisco. There, they were connected with one another and with advisors who were industry experts who knew the ins and outs of their respective projects.

The program was a success, and the founders who graduated hit the ground running. Following its success, the Nex Cubed team recognized that numerous founders were unable to participate but could still benefit from the program. In the fall of that year, Nex Cubed broadened its initiative to include 40 entrepreneurial teams from 16 HBCUs. The demand, need, and value were there, and Nex Cubed formally launched its $40 million Founders Fund to give entrepreneurs from HBCUs pre-seed and seed capital to help launch their promising startups.

Founders are founders, in Evans's view, and have the same basic needs regardless of background. He calls those needs the three C's: customers, capital, and community. The Founders Fund creates a lot of its impact by focusing on the third C, providing mentors, advisors, and people who can guide and support select founders while fostering an environment of collaboration with like-minded entrepreneurs. More important than the business idea is the person behind it. Much of what goes into a startup can be engineered, like a process. However, the special insights and determination of a founder are much harder to find or replicate. Evans's focus was on being married to the problem and not the solution. The founders from HBCUs are often intimately familiar with the problems they're trying to solve, having experienced it in personal and unique ways. The focus was to help them step back and ask, "What does this mean from an overall market perspective?" These founders are already focused on solving these problems. The mental barrier the founders typically struggle with is their sense of scale. Evans and team found that these founders aren't thinking big enough. Investors want to back ideas that offer at least 10 times the return on their investment. Evans helps founders develop that mentality and make their vision bigger.

Evans views investing in minority founders as both a savvy business move and a way to create social impact. Venture capitalists are constantly seeking a distinct advantage. By focusing on overlooked communities, they can tap into a vast pool of talent, obtaining a first-mover advantage by investing early and supporting their growth. In contrast, the majority of investors are vying for a competitive edge within a smaller universe of ideas.

The Founders Fund looks for entrepreneurs who have firsthand experience in the problems they are trying to solve, which happens to align very closely with investments in startups that address areas where African Americans have historically lacked equal access to capital, resources, and services, including financial services, healthcare, education, and housing. The fund backs founders at their earliest stages, starting with ideation and moving through early investment to help them raise more capital from angel investors and other seed funds.

The Venture Studio Model

The HBCU Founders Fund and Nex Cubed are critical to the work at A&T, which Eshelman Innovation branded as PowerUp. The venture studio model combines mechanisms and methodologies that are particularly powerful as a support structure for entrepreneurs from nontraditional, marginalized, or disadvantaged backgrounds.

The venture studio concept originated with Idealab in 1996 and has since spread worldwide because of its effectiveness. Co-author John Bamforth first encountered the approach in Indianapolis. The former co-founders of Indianapolis-based ExactTarget, the venture-backed CRM platform acquired by Salesforce, took their payouts and went to a cabin in the woods to think about the next great business idea they'd pursue together. The debate came down to four or five promising ideas. Rather than pick just one, they decided to find ways to back all four and formed High Alpha Innovation, a successful venture studio that has provided immeasurable insights and experience. Venture studios differ from venture funds, accelerators, incubators, and the like. Instead of seeking entrepreneurs or entrepreneurial ideas to back, venture studios engage directly with problems within organizations and communities. They use empathetic-based, design-thinking methodologies that can evolve a potential idea into a startup. Often, they validate the idea through a minimum viable product or some rigorous due diligence process involving the community, then test the idea in the real world to see if it has some traction in the market. Each venture studio has its secret formula for making its go / no-go decision, but if the light turns green, the studio identifies and recruits entrepreneurs to run and grow those ideas as startups and, hopefully, bring them to scale. Twilio, Bitly, and Moderna are some famous examples of highly successful companies birthed through the venture studio model.

A venture studio has many advantages over a more traditional venture fund, accelerator, or incubator. For the founders or backers of the venture studio, the model allows them to incubate several ideas on parallel tracks while gaining an in-depth, insider's view of the real challenges, barriers, and opportunities of the prospect versus the ones that show up on a PowerPoint deck. They also make all the major decisions involving the launch of that startup, including who its leadership team and board will be, and start with a founder's share of equity rather than a smaller percentage negotiated under a typical funding agreement. Finally, and most importantly, they provide a suite of services to the new company, such as legal, human resources, and marketing.

Why would an entrepreneur or founder be interested in being part of a venture studio–backed startup? Less equity in return for plenty of blood, sweat, and tears? The biggest advantage is the reduction in risk. The founder/entrepreneur gets to step into a situation that's well-vetted, already funded, and positioned to go to market. Plenty of time has already been spent ideating, testing, talking, piloting, pivoting, and selling to get to the point where the startup is ready for capital investment or the market.

Moreover, the founder/entrepreneur doesn't have to bootstrap or forego income until the business has enough capital or revenue to pay a salary; the venture studio pays the entrepreneur and leadership team. This is huge for anyone who might lack the personal resources or flexibility to take the startup leap at a particular time and expand the pool of potential candidates for those leadership roles. Most people, especially mid-career professionals with mortgages and families, might balk at the level of financial pressure and risk that comes with bootstrapping.

The venture itself is also de-risked with success rates not found in traditional accelerators or venture capital models. Eighty-four percent of startups that come out of a venture studio go on to raise seed funding. Seventy-two percent of those make it to Series A, compared to 42 percent of standard startups, and 60 percent go on beyond Series A. According to a report by the Global Startup Studio Network, 30 percent have better results than traditional startups, all while developing a predictable, provable, scalable process for more startups.[6]

The venture studio model provides twice the level of support by offering capital and an experienced team. It grows startups at twice the speed as measured by the time it takes them to reach Series A status—25 months versus the 56-month industry average. Finally, venture studio–backed startups arc twice as likely to make it to a successful exit event, whether that's an acquisition, merger, or IPO (70 percent versus an average of 33 percent for VC-backed companies).

When Eshelman established the PowerUp Initiative with Nex Cubed and the HBCU Founders Fund, all parties saw the advantages of the venture studio model as key to our success and speed. Every investor or backer wants to reduce the risk of an investment and increase the likelihood of strong growth and a significant exit on an accelerated timeline. The venture studio model promised to make that possible. But there were also two other advantages that made the model even more interesting and compelling for our goals.

First is the ability to select the founder and CEO. Every venture studio wants to find the best founder CEO for their startup, and we are no different. But how do you determine who the best founder CEO will be? While the formula may vary from studio to studio, typically selection decisions are based on a mix of relevant experience, past success, technical competencies, entrepreneurial drive, and leadership, among other tangible and intangible factors. All of that makes sense, but it can also perpetuate the kind of limited scope that funds are already guilty of when they make their investment decisions. Likely candidates are no doubt already on their radar screen or within their broader network. What about great candidates who don't have access to that network or are off the grid in some other way?

The team at Eshelman looked into the challenges that Black and other minority entrepreneurs face in gaining access to capital, networks, mentorship, resources, and so on, and saw the venture studio model as the perfect mechanism for facilitating and accelerating the funding of Black or minority-led startups, starting with picking the founder CEO from a broader and more diverse pool of candidates. This is a twist on the venture studio model, as most venture studios do not specifically consider diversity when making their founder-CEO selections.

Another significant advantage in the venture studio model is that it gives us the ability to decide on the market or social needs we want to solve. Eshelman Innovation has focused on needs that present themselves in North Carolina, which is home to the institute. At A&T with PowerUp, the institute has turned its attention to food insecurity and mental health in the African American community, thanks to a significant grant from the Humana Foundation. It has applied a design-thinking approach, often used by venture studios, to identify the needs and challenges involved in getting food-insecure people to a better place. With its methodology, the institute can leverage the ideas and experiences of people who don't always have an entrepreneurial mindset, test them for market need and competition, develop the necessary technology, find the funding, recruit the right CEO founder, and tap the advice, technology, and resources of its partners. This support helps the companies secure pilot and user opportunities as well as more funding to facilitate growth.

Building Trust and Accelerating Change

Eshelman Innovation holds the view that every diverse or marginalized community has unmet market needs, and solutions to those challenges are already embedded in those communities. They also believe that many of those solutions are highly scalable with the right support, enablement, backing, and methodology. They feel a strong duty to accelerate innovation from these communities and drive toward transformative wealth creation for those who participate.

One of the most challenging aspects of this model is gaining and sustaining trust. Many marginalized communities are sensitive to a long history of being used and abused. It's one thing to go into those communities and offer support for translating their needs; it's quite another to develop the kind of trust necessary to cultivate collaborative business partnerships that will include outside stakeholders who might as well come from other worlds. Many in the community are concerned about sharing their ideas, getting cheated, being used, or seeing their input and voices be excluded from the process. They may hesitate to give important feedback or offer better ideas or solutions. This requires more than just showing up and being present; it takes frequent, sustained interaction to develop an ongoing working relationship based on deep familiarity and trust.

It helps to have the right partners, locally and across the board. It helps to work on problems of profound social need. Communities dealing with food insecurity, health inequities, or opioid addiction are usually desperate for outside support, and the very nature of those challenges facilitates a level of vulnerability and emotional storytelling that accelerates connection and sense of shared purpose.

The institute leans on and learns from leaders in these communities. This began with a deliberate effort to bring leaders of color onto the institute's many boards. They were conscious in building an array of talent from many backgrounds to ensure that governance and problem-solving would use multiple lenses. Then, there is the ability to leverage other organizations. With partners such as the Humana Foundation, which have leaders and strategies that align with ours, we could impact health equity through innovation and entrepreneurship. The Humana Foundation was the first to take the bold step of supporting the institute's work at A&T.

Perhaps its best example of leadership to date has come from a dear friend of the institute and board member, Renard Charity, the external face and internal cheerleader for PowerUp. Born and raised in Richmond, Virginia, as the son of two physicians, Charity was drilled to "work hard, study hard, and figure out ways to serve your community" from the earliest age.[7] This was a family mantra that could be traced back to his great-grandmother, who had been the community midwife. Charity's father had also noticed in his formative years that his White neighbors sent their kids to private schools. Once he had earned the opportunity, he decided he would emulate this approach, so Charity and his siblings attended private high school and then Ivy League colleges. He attended Princeton, where he majored in history and played football as a defensive lineman. This was far from the traditional family pursuits of medicine and education. In fact, it was a tough day when he told his father that he was not pursuing medicine but going to Stanford Graduate School of Business. As his father said, "You're breaking the playbook; you're pursuing a profession outside of our community. Can you trust them?"

Charity wondered about it, too. While at Princeton and even afterward, he saw others pursue entrepreneurial ventures, but he wasn't quite ready to pursue similar opportunities. He felt he needed to build his knowledge base and a network. He needed a safety net. He admitted to feeling envious of some of his buddies whose fathers were hedge fund managers. They had access to knowledge, networks, capital, guidance, and a safety net. Although he came from a respectable family, he would have to finance himself. For Charity, it was investment banking and mergers and acquisitions at Morgan Stanley that helped him understand the ropes of business before deciding to attend Stanford.

Fast forward to 2023, Charity has realized his business potential from his roles at BCG and now as managing partner at Fletcher Spaght, a growth strategy firm in Boston. Interestingly, most of his time is dedicated to healthcare innovation, maybe due to his father's influence. His passion for helping his community has not changed, a value that was instilled deeply by his family. He believes it is his duty and obligation to pass on any lessons he's learned to others who want to be successful in business and entrepreneurship. If a southern institution like UNC-Chapel Hill wants to help extend entrepreneurship to underrepresented communities. He's all in.

Charity and other partners at the institute share a number of goals and social concerns. They recognize the need for change and to realize the opportunities in minority communities. Most importantly, they share an urgency, an unwavering impatience insisting that there is no need to wait. They know the time is now!

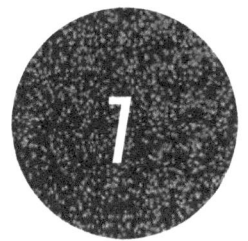

AN OPPORTUNITY TO STIMULATE
INNOVATION IN CORPORATE AMERICA

Co-author John Bamforth spent nearly 30 years of his career at Eli Lilly and Company, and its approach to innovation and advancing talent as part of that commitment was at the heart of his approach to his new role at Eshelman Innovation. The purpose of this chapter is twofold, first to discuss how some of the concepts and observations in the book can be applied to a corporate setting, and second to discuss how one corporation began to understand and embrace ideas of difference into its corporate culture.

Eli Lilly and Company was founded in 1876 by Colonel Eli Lilly, a veteran of the Civil War, who had returned to his chosen profession as a pharmacist. Today, Lilly is now the biggest pharma company in the world (judged by market capitalization) based in Indianapolis with offices in 125 countries.[1] With its roots in pharmacological research and drug manufacturing, Lilly has always been a prominent leader in drug innovation, starting with its development of the anti-malarial medicine quinine in the 1870s, then a range of life-changing drugs over the next century, including insulin for diabetes in the 1920s and Prozac in the 1990s. Most recently, Lilly has become a prominent innovator in a novel portfolio of obesity drugs and one of the first transformative treatments for Alzheimer's disease. Over the last decade, it has doubled down on diverse talent within its executive ranks as a catalyst for improved organizational performance. While that may sound glibly promotional, the process was raw, disruptive, and perspective changing, and it had a profound impact. The Eli Lilly story shows how such innovation can impact individuals and businesses—and benefit us all in the process.

Lilly's work on diverse talent development intensified in 2017 when David Ricks, a 25-year Lilly veteran, was named CEO. No one was surprised by the type of man chosen for the job. The previous CEO, John Lechleiter, had been with the company for over 30 years. As White men with establishment pedigrees, it would seem unlikely for either to initiate meaningful changes to the diversity of the company and the experience of diverse people working for the company. Yet each did.

Despite his own race and gender, Ricks understood the importance of diverse teams. He'd worked overseas in China and Canada in important international roles. His wife was a working physician and parent, juggling the very real challenges of being a woman and mother in a demanding profession. He'd seen and understood the data that showed, very convincingly, the impact of diversity on team performance, even at the most senior levels.

As just one of many examples, according to McKinsey, firms that are highest in racial, ethnic, and gender diversity are 25–36 percent more likely to have financial returns above the industry median. When that diversity is found in the leadership team, the impact is even greater. For such reasons, Ricks believed that increasing diverse talent was not just the right thing to do from moral, ethical, or public-relations perspectives, but the right thing to do from a business perspective, especially when framed in his innovation agenda.

Like any complex business initiative, that effort started with an assessment of the company's current state, and it would ultimately be measured in terms of the impact on organizational performance and competitive advantage.

Before becoming CEO, Ricks had championed research to better understand the experience of women in the company. That research was run by the marketing group, which used the same methodology to understand the needs of women working at Lilly as they used to understand the needs of customers for product development, a process known as *customer journey mapping*. This time, the customer was a woman progressing through her career in the Lilly culture. What was it like for that woman to join the company? What was it like at each level or part of the organization? The initiative and report was called "The Woman's Journey," and its findings were surprising to many men in senior leadership positions. In contrast, it was not surprising to many women. Typically, most women hired by Lilly were extremely excited and enthusiastic to join a successful Fortune 200 company with a global reach and lots of opportunities for career growth. The Woman's Journey research showed that such enthusiasm and optimism peaked at around the five-year mark of a woman's career. From that point forward, most women experienced a steady decline in their positive feelings for the company. This culminated at the senior leadership ranks, where morale, trust, satisfaction, recognition, support, and other measures reached their lowest levels.

When that data was presented to the executive team, it was extremely eye-opening. Senior women leaders were asked to verify it and answered that the characterization of their experience at Lilly was completely accurate. That led to important changes and hard measures of progress, which helped improve the women's journey considerably. When Ricks took over as CEO, he immediately launched a similar initiative to examine the African American journey at Lilly.

Thin Air

One of the few leaders at Lilly who could understand the path personally was Tony Ezell. Ezell was born in Alabama, where 70 percent of residents remain their whole lives. Ezell left the state to work for a company where he often felt set apart. He also became deeply involved in the "work that the company initiated to improve its experience for employees of color."

Ezell was used to standing out. Growing up, there were very few African Americans in his Catholic high school. By his senior year, he was six-foot-two, quarterback of the football team, and president of the student government, the first African American to be elected to that role. Still, he never felt like he fit in. When he went back to his high school for his 35th anniversary, he realized why he'd left the community and most of his classmates had stayed. It wasn't because they lacked ambition, drive, or imagination. Rather, most of them had tapped into networks and social, family, and business opportunities that had not been available to Ezell. Alabama was a state where two very different realities existed side by side, and he was never going to succeed in that environment like his White classmates.

His parents understood and supported his ambitions. His family wasn't poor—his father taught culinary arts, and his mother worked at the community college—but Ezell had to scrounge to get anything extra. He earned money from collecting cans for recycling. He worked at the local McDonald's. He did bookkeeping for his mother. He studied hard and succeeded wildly in academics, earning a National Merit Scholarship. When he interviewed at Florida A&M, a historically Black university, the dean met with him and five other Black male scholarship students. She told them that, despite their success, none of them were special. Florida A&M was filled with superstars just like them. She promised, however, that if they got through the school's program, they would have the education and preparation needed to make their mark on the world. Ezell felt supported by someone in authority for the first time in his life and inspired by what would become possible if he followed the rigorous program the school offered.

After graduating, Ezell was hired as a sales specialist at Lilly. After five years in that role, he joined management as a district sales manager. He steadily climbed the ranks, taking on a new position every two years, gaining responsibility over sales, then different business units, then national marketing, and then global marketing, until he was named chief customer officer for the company. Along the way, he encountered incidents of bias and prejudice, such as the senior executive who told Ezell he was surprised to see what a quick thinker he was. It was difficult for Ezell to interpret this as anything but a presumption that, as an African American, he was more likely to have been a slow thinker.

One of the challenges Ezell experienced was the emotional difficulty of fitting in and being part of the club. He recalls a time when he went golfing with two senior leaders and one junior employee who happened to be White. Ezell saw right away how at ease that junior employee seemed to be, despite the underlying pressure of playing with an influential group of senior executives. Very quickly, this colleague was participating in the little jokes that went back and forth without any apparent awkwardness or concern that he might be putting his reputation and career in jeopardy. It would have required far too much energy for Ezell to do anything like that constantly, but for this junior employee, it was normal.

Because he led marketing, Ezell was very involved in the focus group work during The Women's Journey, and then with The African American Journey, as well as subsequent Journeys for other minority groups. Like the CEO Dave Ricks, he was intrigued because he believed the work would help improve the company's innovation and competitive advantage, not just primp its representational image. He also suspected it would surface a record of experiences similar to his own. But it was difficult to point to such moments and say, "Here's a problem with the company as a whole." The African American Journey work was so effective not only because the stories were so compelling and eye-opening but also because the data validated those stories.

It was clear that Lilly was better than many companies at hiring talented African American employees. The company was also unusual because it made specific efforts to support African American employees by bringing them together at Lilly headquarters once a year. But it was also true that Lilly lost many of those employees two to five years after they came on board because they didn't feel valued or supported. So, what went wrong?

The data helped the marketing group identify specific problems and determine indisputably that they were systemic because they affected interviewing for promotions and succession management. For instance, performance scores obviously affect promotion and succession management. However, through the data, the marketing team could see that the performance assessment document was clearly influenced by how well the scorer knew the person being assessed. Many African American employees did not have the social and networking opportunities of their White peers. So, even though their objective job performance showed high potential, the assessor would give them a lower score on their report. As a result, African Americans with the same job experience and performance record as their White peers would not be promoted as quickly.

That was the kind of situation Ezell had experienced firsthand over the years. If an African American manager was not in the room during performance evaluations, no one would speak up on that employee's behalf to counter the narrative that they did not have the potential to advance. Combined with the qualitative data—videos of people recounting their personal stories—the research created a compelling argument for the need for change.

After the data and the videos of stories had been collected, the results were reported to a group of African American employees for validation. John was one of the few White executives in attendance. He remembers the level of emotion in the room, and the way many in attendance criticized Ezell and other Black leaders for "not doing more" on behalf of others.

Ezell rejected that responsibility. As a leader, it was not his job to "put a thumb on the scale" for Black employees. He needed to remain balanced, objective, and open. He did, however, believe that the value of the findings created an obligation for the company to do something about them, so that's where Tony put his considerable energies.

In the promotion process, for example, they now had justification for assessing African American candidates more closely with a stronger argument for their readiness. That directly affected how quickly Black people got promoted. The impact across the company was deeply meaningful to Ezell. And over the next few years, Ezell saw a culture change, a shift from symbolic gestures during Black History Month, and a movement toward creating real advancement opportunities for those who deserved promotions. African Americans were finally recognized for their performance and contributions to the company. And with these efforts retention numbers also started to improve.

Working for Belonging

Sue Mahony is not Black and was not even American when her tenure at Eli Lilly started. But her lived experience as a woman rising through the ranks of a giant global corporation reinforced the insights shared by the employees we interviewed at Lilly who are Black. As the head of human resources and an independent board director, Mahony has been a mentor to many women in the business and corporate world. (She has been married to co-author John Bamforth for 34 years.) She is passionate about advancing diverse talent. Not too surprisingly, she was very candid in sharing her thoughts on her Lilly experience and more recent experiences with other companies as an independent board director, her more recent role.[2]

Mahony grew up in London, England, but her parents came from County Cork in Southern Ireland. Like many Irish, they moved to England to find work. Mahony remembers her father having multiple jobs in construction, maintenance, and other areas, while her mother became a nurse. Through hard work and discipline, her parents managed to earn and save enough to buy a house, which provided stability and security Mahony would need to get a better education than they had.

From a young age, Mahony never saw her parents just relax at home, reading a book for pleasure. They were always on the go. Her mother loved being a nurse—it was more a vocation than a job—but at home, she didn't slow down. Mahony admired and idolized her mother for her tenacity and energy, but there were aspects of her life that she didn't want to emulate—her insistence on doing all the housework, for example, no matter how tired she might have been, and the guilt she harbored for feeling as if she wasn't doing enough at home or had somehow let the family down for not being around more. Mahony saw it as a mode of female experience that she wanted to step away from. Those patterns went deep, however, and would come out in different ways for Mahony later in life.

She got lucky in her educational opportunities. Though her mother and father had never gone to college, they valued education for Mahony. At her middle school, the top students in the class were invited to apply to grammar school, a high school where students are admitted based on ability. Academically, Mahony was first in her middle-school class but didn't receive the opportunity to apply. Her mother was furious and went to the school to find out why. It turned out that one of the teachers had a daughter in the class who'd been given the opportunity instead. Mahony's mother complained so forcefully that the headmistress overturned the decision and gave the application to Mahony. It was the first and only time she saw her mother take an unbending stance on her education.

Maybe Mahony's mother understood how life-changing the opportunity to go to a top high school would be. It certainly turned out that way for Mahony—and it's one of the reasons she and John share a passion for education to this day and have started a scholarship fund for students from disadvantaged backgrounds.

Out of grammar school, Mahony could go to university, though at first she didn't want to apply. None of her old friends were going, and she felt like university was for other people, including the girls at her grammar school who'd come from private schools. To Mahony, those were the types of students who deserved to go to university. She didn't feel as though she belonged. Once again, it was her mother's influence that won out as she encouraged Mahony to at least apply. True to her working-class roots, she didn't apply to one of the elite schools like Oxford or Cambridge, but to Aston, a college that was more of a technical school. She was also practical in her choice of majors. Her high school teacher had told her that chemistry could lead to a good job in pharmacy or business, so that's what Mahony applied for. She was in Ireland when the news of her acceptance came, and she remembers crying because she felt overwhelmed by the path that lay ahead.

After graduating, she worked at Boots Group, now part of Walgreens Boots Alliance, as a pharmacist. One Sunday morning reading the newspaper, she saw an ad for a PhD student in the cancer research lab at Aston University. She'd never considered such a thing before, but a strange feeling of recognition came over her. Right away, she called a few friends from university and asked them what they thought about her applying. All of them said it sounded like something she'd love, so she applied, got accepted, and found herself back at Aston in the PhD program doing cancer research.

This time, when she completed her studies, the head of cancer research introduced her to a connection at Schering-Plough, the American pharmaceutical company. She made a consequential career choice: Given the option between entering the medical side of the business or the sales side, Mahony went to work in sales. She'd received advice that the medical side of the business had a ceiling for people with PhDs, but that experience in sales would give her more opportunities long term. And she could always move back to medical later if she changed her mind.

When Mahony joined the Schering-Plough sales team in 1989, she was the first and only female sales representative. The men didn't know how to act around her. When she walked into the room for her first meeting, they all stood up because a lady had entered. Although they were polite and nice to her, she was regularly reminded of her gender, like the time her boss asked her to pour tea for the men in the room. There was nothing vindictive about their attitude; it was just the norm. Still, it was clear she was viewed differently and not one of the club.

With her parents' work ethic, there was no question that she'd give it her all. The effort paid off. Two years later, she was recruited by Amgen. The company had just launched operations in the UK and wanted to recruit talented salespeople from other companies. They went to all the top customers and asked who was the best salesperson they'd encountered. Mahony was among them, and Amgen brought her on board as an oncology sales specialist. The new sales team was a small group, and Sue was by far the youngest and least experienced. The UK branch had a startup mentality, however, and it was ready to give people a chance based on their merit, not their seniority.

Once again, her hard work paid off and she was elevated to marketing manager over several more experienced male colleagues. One of them, unable to accept that he'd been beaten by a woman for a job he wanted, blatantly accused Mahony of sleeping her way into the role. Mahony never cracked at work and always kept a tough exterior, but at home, when she and John talked about their days, she'd sometimes burst into tears. She stuck it out, and her success started to earn her credibility with the team and a good reputation in the industry as someone on the rise. After her next stint at Bristol Myers Squibb, she was recruited by Lilly and moved to the United States, succeeding through roles in global brand development and sales, then becoming president of Eli Lilly Canada, senior vice president of the global company, head of human resources, and president of oncology.

Mahony considers herself fortunate to have had the bosses and mentors she had along the way, most of whom were White men. She was very comfortable in all-male environments, having grown up around her brother and his friends, and she had John's experience and insights to help her navigate some of the more perplexing situations and challenges she ran into. The speed of her rise was remarkable, but as someone who would end up leading many people, she recognizes now that her ability to work hard and produce results would have been noticed by any boss. Nevertheless, she never felt ready for any promotions she was offered before she accepted.

She chalks that up now to a deeply ingrained sense of imposter syndrome. It's a phenomenon that she's come across over and over among the women she's worked with and mentored—and one that was also mentioned by the men Lilly interviewed who are Black. She did not notice this same insecurity among most White men she encountered.

According to McKinsey's 2019 Lean In study, women and men tend to be equally recognized at the entry level, but the percentage of women falls to 25 percent at the executive ranks and 7 percent at the CEO level.[3] Kate Purmal, the author of *Composure: The Art of Executive Presence*, explains that many men in the majority have an elevated sense of self-worth from an early age. Women lack this, and as a result, according to Purmal, they tend to respond with more sensitivity and anxiety to signals and reactions from the outside world. External judgments hit them harder and are often interpreted more harshly. Meanwhile, internal judgments (the inner critic) may be even more cutting.[4] This shows up as perfectionism, lack of confidence, and feeling like a fraud, all emotions Mahony can relate to.

Overcoming imposter syndrome and developing a healthy sense of entitlement, self-worth, and confidence can be a lifelong challenge for anyone. That effort is bolstered by the sense of psychological safety that comes from being around colleagues, peers, mentors, or mentees of a similar group or experience. This is aligned with the idea of enclaves. An enclave is a place of psychological safety, where a person of a particular group can relax instead of staying vigilant to fit in, do right, succeed, and blend in or stand out. In enclaves, people can just be themselves. It's not a full-time retreat from the majority world but a place of rest, recuperation, safety, and support to get back out there and engage with forces that may not always be hospitable, nurturing, or even safe.

Mahony was on the executive committee when Lilly launched its Women's Journey research. She was extremely proud of the company for facing questions around gender bias honestly. She also noted the surprise of her male peers at the top when the results were revealed. Hearing the stories and seeing the data, they asked her, "Was that what it was really like for you?" Mahony could answer definitively that the analysis was accurate.

In some ways, however, she was as surprised as her peers that it was such an ongoing reality for younger women. This revelation left her feeling some misplaced Irish guilt. Like her mother, she worried that she hadn't done enough, despite having had many female mentees over the years. They were all going through similar challenges. The situation served as a wake-up call for Mahony. Soon, she had another one. She began to hear rumblings that her female African American colleagues were complaining about the Women's Journey findings because it didn't reflect their experience. To many, it was the White Women's Journey. Mahony was disappointed by their criticism and secretly felt it was misplaced. But when the company later conducted their African American Women's Journey, she came to understand and wondered how she could have been so naïve. She attended the presentation of results and was blown away by how different their journey was compared to hers and her White colleagues'. Asked to speak by one of the presenters, Mahony stood at the back of the room with tears in her eyes and apologized for having blinders to their experience and the unconscious biases she shared with White men. It was an eye-opening lesson she has never forgotten.

All those perspectives inform her work today after leaving Lilly. With her experience as a top executive in the pharmaceutical industry, she has been asked to join many boards. One of her personal requirements for public boards is that she not be the only woman or minority in the room. If the company doesn't have another woman or minority on their board, they're likely not serious about their diversity, equity, and inclusion efforts. And the boards with significant diversity, she has found, are the most enjoyable and effective. Mahony wishes for every board to have at least 50 percent women. Although that's not the current reality, at least the conversations are being had.

Mahony is also trying to support female entrepreneurs, founders, and CEOs of the startup companies she invests in. Those numbers are not high, and the women she meets face real challenges that their White male peers don't. Some of those challenges involve fundraising, forging networks, and building relationships with experienced industry leaders and business customers. But many of the challenges are highly personal. Women often struggle with imposter syndrome and doubts about confidence, and fears about having to sacrifice other aspects of their personal lives, such as having children. If it's lonely at the top, it's even more so if you are a woman or from a minority community. This survival mindset complicates the ability to innovate, lead, and take risks.

The Impact

Has the Journey work had an impact on Lilly's innovation and performance, as CEO David Ricks promised it would? At the time Ricks started, Lilly was ranked eighth in the world among pharmaceutical companies. Today, it's number one in terms of market cap. According to John Bamforth, this is no coincidence. Undoubtedly, innovation and business development have fueled its success, yet Lilly's focus on diverse talent has also played a significant role. The executive committee at Lilly is now more diverse than ever, with nearly an equal representation of men and women. There are many drivers of innovation and performance for a business. Diverse perspectives and psychological safety for people from diverse backgrounds enable the decision-making, learning, and risk-taking that are essential to innovation and growth. Along with companies like Netflix[5] and Fidelity,[6] Lilly is now a leader in both those respects.

The question is: How can we do it faster with even greater impact?

8

EXPANDING THE INNOVATION ZONE

Aisha "Pinky" Cole was born in Baltimore in 1988 to Jamaican immigrant parents. On that day, her father, whom she calls the most brilliant man she's ever known, was sentenced to 30 years in prison for his role as the head of a cocaine distribution ring run out of a nightclub. She credits her father for her entrepreneurial instincts. Her mother was a nightclub singer who took whatever job she could to get by while raising Cole and her brother alone. She credits her mother with her enormous capacity for work, her ability to put herself out into the world, and her hustle and drive.

Even as a child, Cole was an entrepreneur with an uncanny instinct for market demand and the gumption to do something about it. She made frozen drinks and sold them from her home. She'd buy Chicken McNuggets and sell them to her classmates for double the price. While still a pre-teen, she became a promoter, organizing enormous parties, charging entry, and earning thousands of dollars a night, which she would count, lying on the floor, with her mother. After high school, she did not set out to be an entrepreneur but went to college at Clark Atlanta, a historically Black university. She graduated with a degree in communications and tried Teach for America for a year, but it didn't click, so she moved to Los Angeles hoping to become an actor.

She got a few acting jobs as an extra and hustled her way into producing. Though she started to earn a lot of money for a 24-year-old, she wasn't scratching her entrepreneurial itch, so she left LA behind and moved to Harlem to open a restaurant.

She wasn't a chef or a cook, but food was important to her family and her Jamaican Rastafarian heritage, and she had instincts about how to brand and sell it. She'd grown up a vegetarian, eating rice and beans and locally grown vegetables. But at her first restaurant, which she called Pinky's Jamaican and American, she offered jerk chicken and oxtails. In retrospect, that wasn't right for her and her vegetarian beliefs. She was just responding to the market demand for traditional Jamaican food. But she learned a lot about selling. She gave the Jamaican concept her flair, painting the restaurant in bright, bubble-gum colors and churning out attention-getting slogans and menu item names. The business did well and she opened a juice bar next door called Pinky's. Then disaster struck.

One night, the restaurant burned to the ground in a grease fire. Cole had no insurance and no way to finance a rebuild. She lost her apartment, her car, and her boyfriend in short order. So, she left Harlem and headed back to LA to take a production job on an Oprah Winfrey–produced show.

Living in LA, she continued to think about entrepreneurial ideas. She read self-help business books voraciously. She also decided to turn wholly vegan and soon realized the options for vegan food were very limited, even in LA, especially at late-night restaurants and hang-out spots after clubbing. She saw a need in the marketplace for a hip vegan experience that would appeal to people like herself.

She moved back to Atlanta for another TV show but kept thinking about ideas for a vegan concept restaurant. The brand was the most important element for her because it organized everything else—the look and feel, a market need, a purpose, and a strategy for bringing the concept to scale. When the name Slutty Vegan popped up during a brainstorming session, she knew she had something. It was provocative, memorable, and sexy—and sex sells. The brand became the galvanizing force.

She did not even yet know what kind of food Slutty Vegan would offer, but she continued to come up with provocative names for dishes as she mulled the possibilities. Timing and opportunity collided to produce some luck. New plant-based meat substitutes were becoming hot items, especially Impossible Burgers, which eager consumers would seek out in restaurants and stores, even as supply couldn't keep up with demand. She realized a vegan burger was the perfect idea and developed Slutty Vegan's first burger and fries. She came up with the recipes for the special sauce and fry seasoning herself and offered take-out orders through an app that delivered through Uber Eats.

Sales were slow to non-existent at first. Then, a vegan friend with a social network following promoted her brand, and the business changed overnight. Suddenly, Slutty Vegan was hip, and its brand appeal and recognition started to resonate. To build on that momentum, Cole sought out celebrity endorsements in the hip-hop community and got a plug from Snoop Dogg that went viral on her Instagram page. Demand skyrocketed. In short order, she put $10,000 down on a food truck and opened a brick-and-mortar restaurant just four months later in a historically Black neighborhood in Atlanta a few blocks from Martin Luther King, Jr.'s, childhood home. She was 30 years old.

In the five years since, she's raised $25 million and expanded her Slutty Vegan brand of restaurants to 11 more locations in Dallas, New York City, and Birmingham. She launched her own line of salsas and dips, sold in Targets around the country, and wrote a vegan cookbook. She's also spun off a few related concept restaurants and developed a massive social media following that keeps her momentum going. She now operates a $100 million business, and has a reasonable path forward to a billion-dollar operation.

How did Cole do it? In a way, her story, like that of any self-made entrepreneur, is both ordinary and unique. She has an iconic presence, brand savvy, uncanny marketing instincts, and the drive of a Steve Jobs, Richard Branson, or Martha Stewart. She also ticks off some boxes for how innovators from non-mainstream communities become successful.

For example, she illustrates how diversity in experience, personality, background, and outlook is not a detriment to success but drives innovation. In other words, her identity and life experience informed her entrepreneurial journey in important ways. She drew on her own family upbringing and cultural heritage, not only for her entrepreneurial skills and business instincts, but also for the concept of selling vegan food. She saw a marketplace demand that might have easily gone overlooked in the mainstream—young Black people with disposable income who had a strong desire for vegan food. She leaned on her various enclaves to germinate that idea and accelerate its development, launching in a Black neighborhood, networking with hip-hop and Instagram influencer friends, and getting support from the vegan community. She had the empowered impatience to pursue those ideas not years from now, not after she'd gotten education and experience as a chef or restauranteur, not after she'd secured the right financing or backing or support, but immediately. She'd pushed through challenges and discovered what she needed to figure out in the process. She also knew that this idea cooked up for one market, one demographic, and one neighborhood would have scalable appeal. That not just Black people, but all people, would benefit.

The most amazing thing about Cole's story is that, despite all the barriers to success for a Black woman in the restaurant business, and the uniqueness of her flare and personality, she made entrepreneurial success look ordinary, a path that can be understood and followed.

Purpose-Driven and Diversity-Driven Prosperity

Discussions based on differences often prompt strong reactions today. In particular, there's a lot of resistance now to the idea that people of diverse backgrounds warrant or deserve special consideration. But the innovation story of diversity is not a right or left, Republican or Democrat issue. Diversity-driven innovation benefits everyone because social progress and economic development are not a zero-sum game. Competition may feel like a sport with winners and losers, but in economic growth, we all do better when the greatest number of people succeed. Diversity can drive prosperity in an accelerated way when there are certain conditions and support structures in place: a sense of safety, shared resources, community.

Consider the story of Lewiston, Maine, as an example of the transformational impact that minority communities can have on majority communities. Today, Lewiston is infamous for a mass shooting spree in 2023 that left 18 people dead, but the city has a rich history. It sits on the Androscoggin River in central Maine, about two-and-a-half hours north of Boston by car. As in Rocky Mount, North Carolina, the first White settlers arrived to farm and built a few sawmills. The locals knew the river and its falls could be tapped for power and attempted to build some dams and canals to operate larger mills, but they couldn't find the capital to fund the projects. In the 1880s, some investors from Boston finally came forward to finance a canal system, enabling Lewiston to join the textile mill revolution sprouting up around New England. The prosperity that resulted continued through the early 1900s. Then, the tide began to turn.[1]

Labor and material costs made textile production prohibitively expensive in New England. The bottom fell out of the market as new competition arose overseas. The mills began closing in the mid-1950s, and a long period of decline set in. Unemployment rose. Economic growth stopped. The population began to fall, dropping by 15 percent between 1970 and 2000. By then, the city was part of the poorest region in Maine.

Lewiston's story is not unique in America. Over those 30 years, many communities across the country experienced social decline and economic upheaval. Industries transitioned. Trade agreements shifted high-paying labor to other countries where pay was lower. Government investment tightened. Global finance patterns affected everything from personal loans to housing markets in mysterious ways. Substance use increased. Health declined. The population got older as young people moved elsewhere. All those macroeconomic forces made it harder to thrive.

Unlike many of those communities, however, Lewiston found a way to revitalize itself. Starting in 1999, it took in more than a thousand Somali refugees from various resettlement locations around the country. When they first arrived in America, many of those refugees had been given low-rent apartments with little prospect for improving their life status. They looked elsewhere and learned about Lewiston, which had good schools and affordable housing.

The mayor at the time wanted to discourage this migration, fearing the drain on social services, so he wrote an open letter to the Somali community requesting that they stop coming. This provoked strong reactions both for and against the mayor. Those who disagreed with the mayor spoke out against his anti-immigrant sentiment, but others felt the same way and began a series of protests against the Somali arrivals. Tensions continued to rise, and Lewiston soon became a battleground for pro and anti-immigrant viewpoints. In 2003, a group of White supremacists from Illinois showed up. In response, 4,000 people, including Republican senators Olympia Snowe and Susan Collins, formed a counterprotest. Public sentiment shifted toward the immigrants, and more continued to arrive, including a secondary wave in 2005 of Somali Bantus, a separate ethnicity from the previous Somalis.

As a result, Lewiston became one of the fastest-growing communities in Maine. Instead of adding to the social burden of the community, the Somali immigrants contributed to its turnaround. Crime declined. Economic growth resumed. Rents, which had been plummeting, stabilized.

One of those new residents was a man named Hussein Ahmed. Like many of his fellow refugees, he'd left Somalia as a young person to escape war and violence. At first, he'd lived in a refugee camp in Kenya, then came to the United States in 2001. In 2002, he joined others from the Somali community in relocating to Lewiston, Maine, where he opened a store. Through his store, Ahmed runs several businesses, ranging from an interpreter service to a tax service and a money transfer service, whatever people need. He's also gotten married, and he and his wife have five children. He's attending college to earn his bachelor's degree.[2]

Like Ahmed, many Somali refugees have opened their own businesses in previously abandoned buildings: cafés, travel agencies, grocery stores, restaurants, clothing shops, even a mosque. Much like Rocky Mount's Reuben Blackwell, a new generation of civic leaders emerged to develop the social capital of the area and promote education, independence, and business development. Fatuma Hussein, who came to the United States at age 11, founded United Somali Women of Maine to promote gender equality and help improve opportunities for young women.[3]

Somalis have also taken up farming. In Somalia, farming was always considered low-caste work because it was forced upon them by colonists or strong-arm rulers. In America, however, the Somalis found that farmers are often respected as leaders of their communities. As Bantu Somalis settled around the country, they began to farm to provide themselves with fresh, healthy produce. This had a powerful impact. Many refugee groups are susceptible to declines in health because of their sudden consumption of fast food as a major part of their diets. The Somali refugees saw their health improve. Recognizing this, the USDA began to fund programs promoting local farming among immigrant communities. Farming is now a common occupation for the Somalis of Maine.[4]

Minnesota also experienced its own wave of Somali immigrants starting in the early 2000s. Today, there are over 86,000 Somalis in the state, the most in the nation. By 2008, Somali refugees had started over 550 new businesses. In 2021, four Somali nurses started their own business to provide stable housing to people with high-risk health conditions. After raising grants from city and state agencies and loans, they bought a local apartment building and refurbished it for disabled or in-need patients. Their aid keeps these patients from emergency departments, hospital readmissions, and local shelters, saving significant expenditures.

Salman Elmi, who came to Minnesota with his parents, started his own business to inspire others in his community to do the same.[5] In 2019, he co-founded Tavolo, an AI-driven analytics platform that enables restaurant marketing. He and his co-founders drew on experiences working in their own family-owned restaurants. In 2021, Tavolo was named Emerging Startup of the Year,[6] and in 2023 it got backing from Techstars as the first local participant in the Farm to Fork Accelerator.[7]

Hilal Ibrahim came to Minneapolis as a young girl from California. In 2017, when she was 22, she founded Henna & Hijabs, a company that designs tailored hijabs that are healthy, practical, and fashionable. Her high-fashion line of hijabs sells through Nordstrom. In 2019, she designed the first medical-grade hijabs for Twin Cities' hospitals, a line she expanded to markets all across the country. In 2023, the site leader of a local Amazon warehouse reached out to Ibrahim to ask her to develop a hijab specifically for warehouse work. Henna & Hijabs designed a line of hijabs with highly breathable fabric and lengths cut to avoid workplace accidents. As Asad Aliweyd, executive director of the New American Development Center put it, "This shows our young Somali Americans who were born and raised in this country [they] can bring their businesses into the mainstream level. We need more of this."[8]

Falling in Love with the Problem

Shuchin Shukla would be the first to insist that he doesn't represent the rural, impoverished, primarily White communities of Appalachia that he serves as a doctor specializing in family medicine, public health, and addiction, but his own story and his impact on those communities feel as unlikely and inspirational as a Hollywood movie.

He grew up in Saint Charles Parish, Louisiana, a community of 50,000 a few miles west of New Orleans. Both his parents immigrated from India. His father was a scientist and his mother was a pediatrician who mostly worked with Medicaid patients. Though the family experienced a lot of overt and subtle racism during Shukla's childhood, his mother was also well-known in the community and he remembered getting a lot of attention as her son. Being Indian and the son of a doctor set him apart as a lifelong outsider.

Like many second-generation immigrant children, Shukla had contradictory impulses. He studied hard in school because he knew what was expected of him, but he also had a rebellious streak. He felt restless and angst-ridden as someone who did not fit in with his own family or the Black and White groups at school. The academic side of him won out, and he secured a coveted spot in a math and science high school. Surprisingly, he also felt more at ease in that environment. For the first time, he wasn't completely alone. Instead, he was surrounded by other marginalized students. Some of them were Asian or South Asian. Some were alternative in look, lifestyle, or gender preference. Shukla could relate to their angsty take on life, and it helped him develop confidence that he could find safety in his enclave and grow from there.

From there, he went to Tulane University. Though it was still in New Orleans, the new enclave broadened his horizons and perspective further. He became energized by ideas around social justice and the potential of marginalized groups to create social change. And his own life path was beginning to become clearer. He knew he wanted to be a doctor and to serve in public health. After four undergraduate years at Tulane, he started medical studies there in 2005.

Three weeks after the school year began, Hurricane Katrina hit. When the levees broke, he joined others trying to bring support and care to displaced people, distributing food, finding medical supplies, setting up generators, even breaking into an abandoned nursing home to find a working dialysis machine. For Shukla, it felt like a real-time laboratory for social justice, community building, and aid delivery. It was also one of the most engaging and influential experiences of his life. He saw how the suffering and pain of a community ran along the fault lines of race, gender, and poverty, and how social justice and healthcare are intertwined. In his academic studies, he was inspired by the way physician faculty members lived their principles through their clinical work.

For his residency program, he chose to go far afield, to the Bronx, which had one of the strongest traditions of public health in the country. The diversity of his new community—80 percent non-White, 50 percent non-native English speaker—and its vibrant cultural life was thrilling to be around. His residency program in family and social medicine helped him focus on the kind of marginalization, trauma, and addiction that shaped and was shaped by social determinants of health and affected personal health, wellness, and happiness. In addition to all that, he met his future wife.

His first job out of the residency program was in the South Bronx at a federally qualified health center (FQHC) that served a patient population with high rates of HIV, hepatitis C, and various addiction disorders. His work was on the leading edge of new treatments that weren't widely available despite the prevalence of such health issues across the country. Through that work, he began to develop even more empathy for the afflicted. He saw substance use disorder (SUD) as a tool people used to cope with the dark side of American consumerism and the sexual, racial, economic, or violent trauma they'd experienced. He could relate to their sense of marginalization and their contradictory cravings for control and rebellion, and the desire to both fit in and stand apart. He also loved his work.

After he and his wife had their first child, they realized New York would be a challenging place to raise a family and began to look for another place to live. They uprooted their lives and moved to Asheville, North Carolina, in 2017, where his wife had been born and raised. It was a big change culturally for Shukla, but it became quickly apparent that his training in addiction, family medicine, and public health would be of use in the Appalachian communities of western North Carolina. He began working for a clinic that treated a lot of HIV patients and soon expanded his practice to serve addiction patients in other outlying hospitals.

The opioid epidemic had devastated those communities and destroyed many lives. A few years later, the COVID-19 pandemic only made those problems worse. Western North Carolina is not alone. Across the country, 3 million people have had or currently suffer from opioid use disorder. In 2021, there were over 181,000 recorded non-fatal overdoses and 105,000 deaths. In North Carolina in 2021, 2,634 people died, and the combined costs of healthcare, criminal justice, economic productivity, and societal harm cost the state $6.8 billion annually.

This is where Shukla and the team at Eshelman Innovation intersect. As part of a group seeking investment opportunities for socially supportive and innovative ventures, the institute set out to better understand the opioid crisis in western North Carolina. Out of that understanding, it hoped to match problems with solutions and determine whether venture-studio–backed startups could help bring those solutions to scale.

The institute started by listening. A team of people from several organizations, including Eshelman Innovation, High Alpha, Mountain Area Health Education Center, Dogwood Health Trust, and other community organizations, spent six months in Asheville meeting with local care providers, and representatives from government, law enforcement, community-based organizations, and so on. This could have been a performative exercise, the kind of show coastal funders, business leaders, and politicians put on when they want to demonstrate the sincerity of their interest. But we were there to listen, learn, discuss, and forge trusting relationships with people who were deeply involved with the problem and understood the nuances of helping those needing support.

Through that experience, we fell in love with the opportunity, too, and the institute used its analytical capabilities to break it down, identifying key components, gaps, and surface needs. Once the problem was diagnosed thoroughly, the team convened a group of passionate experts to conduct a one-week sprint of intense brainstorming and collaboration, no distractions allowed. The goal was to work through the problem's permutations and develop a business idea to address them. That process worked because we spent a significant amount of time building relationships with those involved and understanding their challenges on the ground.

Shukla was one of the medical experts recruited to bring deep personal insight and experience to the process. Though an outsider himself, he had some reservations at first about meeting with people who were neither part of his adopted community nor experienced experts in healthcare or addiction, despite their good intentions. But he was quickly charged up by the intellectual engagement of the innovation process and could tell that the sprint's leaders cared deeply about the opioid problem. They hadn't shown up with any preconceived solutions or answers. Instead, they asked smart questions and challenged assumptions from multiple angles. Shukla could feel himself catching the innovation bug.

The group identified two points in the patient care journey that present opportunities for providing extra support. One is the period after treatment begins with the person with opioid use disorder. Finding and keeping a job, in particular, is hard, and employers might not have the resources or understanding to provide supportive work environments. But without employment, people often fall back into addictive behaviors.

The other opportunity in the care journey is the period immediately after someone overdoses. It's at this point that a person with opioid use disorder is most likely to seek or accept treatment. This is the "golden hour." When someone raises their hand for help and asks for care, they must be met with resources, compassion, and clinically appropriate responses, or they're almost certain to resume using soon after. Without that intervention, the risk of death through overdose increases dramatically, particularly within the first month. Indeed, it's estimated that about one in 20 people who are discharged after receiving medical treatment in an emergency department for an overdose die within a year. About two-thirds of those deaths can be linked to another opioid overdose.

Most don't get the treatment and support they need at that critical moment for a complex mix of reasons. Resources are constrained. There's stigma associated with addiction and overdosing. Law enforcement, EMTs, and ER staff may lack the time, empathy, perspective, and training to provide the right kind of support in the right way. Overdoses not only devastate lives, but they also put a tremendous financial and human strain on healthcare providers and communities. Finding a way to improve that situation could also improve health, save lives, reclaim potential, save resources for other needs, and help communities and families heal.

For Sprint Week, the team's challenge was to determine how to enable municipalities to implement compassionate, fast, effective, peer-based responses to opioid overdoses. Currently, the region's Emergency Services Sector (ESS) responds to overdoses. The ESS is a community of millions of highly skilled, trained personnel, along with physical and digital resources, that provide a wide range of prevention, preparedness, response, and recovery services during both day-to-day operations and in response to incidents. The ESS includes geographically distributed facilities and equipment in both paid and volunteer capacities organized primarily at the federal, state, local, tribal, and territorial levels of government, such as city police departments and fire stations, county sheriff's offices, Department of Defense police, fire departments, and town public works departments. The ESS also includes private sector resources, such as industrial fire departments, private security organizations, and private emergency medical services providers.

Given the numerous response resources for overdose victims, they are often under strain and unable to adequately meet the needs of people who've overdosed. To create another entry point for care, many communities and regions have turned to a new intervention model delivered by post-overdose response teams (PORT teams). These teams follow up with patients who have experienced an overdose within 72 hours. Then, they try to connect the patient with appropriate care ranging from harm reduction services to treatment to recovery support.

PORT teams are utilized in various ways across the country, but they have a few standard practices. Unlike traditional emergency response services, PORT teams specialize in mental health and substance use. Team members are trained in skills like motivational interviewing to help them understand what a person with SUD might need. They can identify patients who may be open to care and point them in the right direction while providing helpful resources to those who may not be ready to pursue treatment yet. They serve as an emerging strategy to meaningfully engage with people who have experienced overdose.

Perhaps most significantly, PORT teams are peer-led. This means that a person who has recently overdosed will be visited by someone who knows what that experience is like and has the credibility and lived experience to offer unbiased, helpful care. They can be "more casual," "less intimidating," and more willing and able than traditional EMTs to sit with a person and listen to their needs—all critical for gaining patient trust.[9] That approach is also cost effective. Using peer services as part of treatment generates cost savings of $5,494 per individual per year in Georgia.[10] Individuals enrolled in peer support crisis intervention cost Medicaid $2,138 less than Medicaid-enrolled individuals who do not receive peer support.[11] At an FQHC in Colorado, every $1 spent on peer services returns $2.28 in medical savings.[12]

Communities across North Carolina have put resources into PORT teams to help people who've recently overdosed. Recognizing the effectiveness of that model, efforts were made to explore ways to assist municipalities in expanding their utilization. The progression from understanding the issue to proposing a solution led to the conception of a nationwide network of peer responders dispatching on-site teams to communities requiring external assistance for overdose incidents. The potential for these teams to integrate technology and standardized procedures in delivering empathy and evidence-based care to individuals suffering from SUD was evident, instead of pushing them toward healthcare facilities where they may not want to be. Some foresight played a part in developing user-friendly software for responders to quickly onboard patients and identify their needs, enabling them to focus on the person, not the system. The gathered data could be analyzed to improve overdose responses, resource utilization, engagement, and post-overdose interventions.

The team sketched out a go-to-market strategy. They looked to existing PORT teams and EMS services as their initial market to build and test the model, putting together a trial program with one of the local counties to create tools that solve unique PORT needs. The plan is to expand that model to additional Appalachian states and for other use disorders or health conditions that are best treated in the community but are neglected due to barriers (e.g., often transportation). Next, a capital-intensive strategy will be employed to build out PORT teams in cities without the resources to set up their own program and scale the training of deployed teams to alleviate the pressure on emergency services. In the longer term, our primary target customers are Medicaid managed-care organizations (MCOs) and health plans that service Medicaid. The goal is to prove the value of the solution, which is calculated between $2,000 to $5,000 in reduced care costs per patient, and capture a portion of costs saved for the customer.

Goldie was chosen as the company name, referencing the golden hour. Upon realizing the business could be viable, the company hired a temporary CEO to take it to the next level. Amazon, one of the company's partners, supplied a chief technology officer to help build the platform. Shukla is Goldie's informal chief medical officer, helping develop its processes and protocols. His level of talent and commitment could not have been recruited without a hands-on, deeply embedded approach to ideation and problem-solving.

The Goldie team achieved a great deal in a short period. But it was only possible because of the venture-studio system Eshelman Innovation had at the ready, and the goodwill and understanding developed through months of relationship building with local experts. Shukla was crucial to those efforts. His life and career have been informed by his own outsider perspective, which he brought to his work in the Appalachian region. He did ride-alongs with PORT teams, EMTs, police, and other first responders, experiencing the challenges of finding and getting people into an intervention program. He shared a story about riding with an ESS team on the highway when someone noticed a flash of color through the trees. To their trained eye, this meant there could be a tent there. Shukla joined the team in walking through the woods until they came across an encampment with people who needed medical care and likely had substance use disorders. That experience left him with a visceral understanding of how pervasive opioid disorder is in Appalachia, hidden to most of us but clearly in plain sight.

Indeed, the need for addiction services is growing, not slowing, and it's already beyond the capacity of the healthcare system. Shukla was quick to grasp how much a scalable, sustainable digital platform and a business model could support difficult intervention fieldwork. Like many innovators who see a persistent need, he had become tired of waiting for solutions. And as a scientist, he's already excited by the results of those efforts. The data is still early, but the virtual PORT team approach is having a significant impact on survivorship.

An important aspect of this story is the larger impact on the community beyond the support given to people with opioid use disorder. For example, the unexpected enthusiasm of the software programmers working on the Goldie platform was palpable. Immersed in the project's purpose-driven ethos, they found themselves captivated by the Appalachian region's scenic beauty and the unique lifestyle it offered them. Rather than going back to the Midwest or the coasts after the initial product development phase, many chose to stay in North Carolina and help build a real tech ecosystem in Asheville where one did not exist before. That's part of the long-term value of entrepreneurial endeavors. They stimulate more innovation while making communities more prosperous.

Diversity Powers Innovation That Benefits Us All

The experiences of the Somali communities in Maine and Minnesota reflect many different communities and marginalized groups all over the United States. The Hmong Vietnamese or Ukrainian communities come to mind, where the same kinds of stories can be found. Consider Native Americans, like Amber Buker and Richard Chance, from the Choctaw and Cherokee Nations, respectively, who live in Oklahoma and developed Totem, a digital banking app designed for Native Americans to "strengthen a 'new tradition' of Native wealth building" and provide culturally relevant financial products, education, and streamlined access to tribal benefits.[13] Likewise, the story of providing addiction services in Appalachia could be told from the vantage of other communities across the country, rural and urban.

If the very idea of innovation is to bring a new perspective to a stuck problem or underappreciated opportunity, then diversity is a powerful tool for seeing new solutions. Diverse entrepreneurs, often driven by their own life experiences, see and appreciate the need for solutions in areas that others would overlook. They often have an extra sense of mission beyond just wealth generation. They bring the oldest cliché of entrepreneurship to life: They truly want to make the world a better place, more reflective and accepting of their own reality, that lets them and their loved ones thrive—a place that feels like home.

More often than one might expect, these specialized products and services expand into other markets and become mainstream, as fashions change or other customers recognize the value themselves. The expansion of such innovation into the mainstream is powerful proof of our shared human condition, and the capacity of entrepreneurial goods and services to create pathways and win hearts and minds.

The pursuit of happiness or rather, the pursuit of self-actualization and personal attainment is a constant theme in this book. The people in these stories are driven by the ability to own their labor and the value they create instead of having it owned by others. But that pursuit of individual happiness, especially in diversity-powered innovation, is easily woven into the larger sense of purpose around community prosperity. The purpose can come from identity—cultural, personal, historical, and community. And it can give back in a uniquely powerful way to reinforce identity and propagate prosperity.

Diversity-based innovation can solve many of the most difficult problems our country and world face. Imagine if minority communities or marginalized peoples were thought of, first and foremost, as solutions to problems rather than as burdens.

The Pitch

There is considerable resistance to diversity-based innovation. Much of that resistance is rooted in fear—fear of the other, losing ownership, or being diminished, disempowered, or marginalized. This fear is not unique to White Americans. It's endemic to all majority groups, even to minorities when a new minority comes along. Change can be threatening because familiar rules and customs no longer provide a sense of security, safety, and status.

Every step forward can cause a reactionary pushback. The initial embrace of refugees after a great calamity often seems to cause resentment in the aftermath. The prosperity of Black Americans post–Civil War was met by the destruction of Black Wall Streets all over the country.

The task of solving large societal challenges can feel hopeless because the problems seem too big and intractable. One of the virtues of entrepreneurialism is that it starts small and creates a solution that grows in impact and gains broader acceptance. It doesn't have to solve every problem, or even the deepest problems; it only needs to solve a very specific problem, often a very practical or surface-level problem; in the process, a solution can have an outsized impact. Like art, entrepreneurship can be uniquely personal, niche, marginal, and universal at once.

As we near the conclusion of this book, a few more stories emerge that illustrate all of the principles described herein. Let us return to Marcus Whitney, the visionary behind Jumpstart Nova (Chapter 6) and the author of the letter to colleagues in the medical industry that inspired the term "empowered impatience." This story is about his instrumental role in bringing a professional soccer team to Nashville.

Soccer is the world's most popular sport. Until relatively recently, it was an afterthought in American professional sports, relegated to youth leagues, college play, and immigrant communities. Mainstream interest began to grow in the 1990s, especially after the United States hosted a FIFA World Cup game in 1994. Major League Soccer, a professional league, launched in 1996. Whitney was one of many young people who played soccer in high school, but he didn't grow to love the game until he came to Nashville and learned more about its "supporter culture" or "football fan culture," which brings ardent fans and rooting communities together with special chants and traditions.[14] It's the very metaphor of a grassroots or market-driven culture.

The Nashville Metros were Nashville's first soccer team. They played in the Professional Development League, a pro-am league. They were founded in 1998 by a couple passionate about soccer, but folded in 2012, leaving a void for fans. A local follower named Chris Jones decided to start a fan-owned and -operated team called the Nashville FC, which ended up playing in the National Premier Soccer League, a sanctioned amateur soccer league. Official supporters of the Nashville FC had to pay a $75 registration fee for a scarf, a membership card, and voting rights. Whitney

EXPANDING THE INNOVATION ZONE

was member number 89. In its first season, Nashville FC surprised its fans by making the playoffs and winning a round.

Though those fans were few, they were intensely committed to their team and soccer. As their numbers grew, Jones and Whitney started talking on Twitter, sharing their enthusiasm and their "assumed potential" for the venture. Whitney had many questions for Jones and after the season ended, they met for lunch. Jones quickly realized that Whitney brought more to the table than just passion; he also had deep connections in the business community (his enclave), a record of entrepreneurial success, and lots of funding experience. So, Jones asked Whitney to join the fan-based board as chairman. Whitney accepted and focused immediately on upgrading the organization's business operations, technology, and customer management systems. The board's new vision was to bring a professional soccer team to Nashville within 10 years. Why did Whitney want to do this? He loved soccer, he loved the passion of fans for a marginalized but rising sport, he loved being part of that group himself, and he loved the way soccer brought different people in the community together in their shared joy. It was another kind of enclave for people who might otherwise not connect.

As in every high-risk, high-reward journey, complications came fast and often. First, representatives of a professional soccer team from Pennsylvania came to Nashville looking for a new home. Whitney and Jones sprang into action, lobbying the mayor and making their case in local newspapers to let Nashville develop its own team. The board knew it had to bring the team to the pro level to keep its momentum going and fend off outsiders. That required getting the backing of an investor group. Whitney put on his fundraising hat, made up a pitch deck, and met with people in his network. One of them was David Dill, the president of Lifepoint Health, and someone Whitney knew well. Dill was interested in joining the effort and brought a health tech entrepreneur named Chris Redhage onto the team. Dill and Redhage worked side by side with Whitney and Jones for the next eight months, trying to determine the right path to turn the team pro.

The biggest question was: Which league should the Nashville FC join? The USL was the nation's third-division league, but their business model and approach to growing the game appealed to the Nashville team, so that's the league they chose. Elevating the Nashville FC team to pro status required a formal investment group, led by Dill, to take over the club. Dill wanted Whitney to join the new ownership group ("enable ownership"), which required him to resign as chairman of the fan-led board. Though he knew this path would help him achieve the dream of a pro soccer team, it was still a tough decision for Whitney because he loved being part of the fan group.

With his unique lens on the "problem," Whitney recognized the critical importance of that fan support. Accordingly, he lobbied for making the nonprofit group part of the new ownership group, as a way of maintaining that connection to the original supporters. There was precedence for this in the USL. The Seattle team also had allotted a percentage of equity to a supporter trust. With a 1 percent equity stake in the new franchise, and the knowledge that professional soccer was on its way, 96 percent of the members of the Nashville FC fan group voted in favor of selling the rights to the team to the new investor group. As a result, the USL awarded Nashville a professional soccer franchise. The supporter group got to lead the mayor into the arena to make the announcement, singing and cheering along the way.

Only a day later, the local newspaper reported that two prominent Nashville political and business leaders, Bill Hagerty and Will Alexander, intended to bring their own professional soccer franchise to the city. Whitney and his group tried to block out this noise as they got to work establishing their franchise, which required changing the team name from the Nashville FC to the Nashville SC for trademark reasons. When that early flurry of activity settled, the group met with Hagerty and Alexander to discuss their plans. Hagerty and Alexander informed them that they knew Nashville had a real shot to bring a Major League Soccer expansion franchise to the city. MLS is the premier league in the country, so this opportunity would be a dream come true for everyone. But an MLS expansion team required an investment group with deep enough pockets and connections to make a sizable bid and fund a new soccer stadium.

The Nashville SC ownership group turned to John Ingram, the billionaire head of the Ingram Group and an early investor in Whitney's Jumpstart Foundry. Ingram shared their vision and applied his resources to help "accelerate transformative" change. Like Whitney and Dill, he saw a Major League Soccer team as a unifying force and common rallying cry for the city. In line with that, Ingram and his investment group decided to forge an alliance with Whitney and Dill's investment group and form a common front. So, Nashville SC sold a controlling interest in the team to Ingram.

Twelve ownership groups representing 12 cities submitted bids for a new Major League Soccer franchise. Nashville was considered the longest shot of the group. To reinforce the bid, the mayor quickly backed Ingram's plan for a new stadium, and the city approved a $275 million financing package. The new investment group led by Ingram put forward a $150 million offer for the franchise rights, a sum that would have been unimaginable to the fans who founded Nashville FC a few years earlier. Just before Christmas of 2017, MLS announced that Nashville would be chosen for an expansion franchise.

The dream had become a reality. The first Nashville SC Major League Soccer game was played in February 2020 in front of 60,000 ecstatic fans.

Perhaps there could be no more fitting metaphor for the benefits of diversity-driven innovation. Out of unique experiences and perspectives comes recognition of opportunity and passion for bringing it to life. That passion is shared intensely within a niche market (fans), which provides the idea (and the innovators) with enough momentum and support to continue to grow. Obstacles are overcome by reaching out for partnership, in ever-widening circles of support. That partnership is not based on charity but on mutual benefit and shared passion, so it creates a more durable infrastructure for the project. This larger effort builds still more momentum and pathways to resources like financial and political capital. And when the project succeeds, the benefits are shared widely. The fans, the investors, the players, the city, the league, the nation, and even the world have benefitted in small and large ways by the establishment of a viable soccer franchise in Nashville, Tennessee.

The chain of events (starting small and growing large) that led to that achievement could never be predicted or planned. Still, the opportunities for other chains of events and other achievements are limitless and all around us.

We need only open the door.

The Research

There is a growing body of research that demonstrates the value of diversity in innovation and performance. Anyone looking for certainty will be disappointed because the research is nuanced, and the nuance matters. While some of the most consequential research is highlighted here, there are many more studies to engage with for serious students of this work.

Diversity Drives Innovation and Performance

The most popular research cited in the press is a McKinsey study titled "Diversity wins: How inclusion matters."[15] The authors evaluate the racial, ethnic, and gender makeup of companies and then evaluate those companies' financial returns against the median for their industry. The authors attempt to measure whether diverse companies have better financial performance. Their answer is a resounding yes. Diverse companies are 25–36 percent more likely to perform above the industry median. The criticism of this work largely centers on other academics being unable to reproduce their work. McKinsey responded by recreating it themselves, but stopping there would be a mistake. There is plenty more research in multiple domains to consider, only some of which is covered here. One study reviewed the diversity of leadership teams and evaluated both their financial performance and innovation by measuring the number of product launches and innovation efficiency.[16] The study found that companies with an above-average diversity in leadership teams had 9 percent greater earnings before income tax and performed 19 percent better on innovation metrics. This seems to independently confirm and extend McKinsey's findings.

The research also suggests that academia sees a positive benefit. In a Harvard study, a review of millions of US-based scientific papers found that ethnically diverse co-authors (in the United States) were cited more frequently and published in higher-impact publications.[17] This suggests two things. First, an academic is more likely to get into a more prestigious journal when publishing with an ethnically diverse US-based co-author. For those outside of academia, publishing in a high-impact journal is academic currency for tenure and prestige. Second, the higher citation rate suggests an increased quality of research. More citations suggest that your ideas are more widely recognized by academic peers and built on across fields. In other words, the publication is more ground-breaking and innovative, resulting in higher H-index scores, the most reliable and robust metric for academic scholarship. Clearly, it is not only minorities benefitting from more diversity.

Another view of how majority populations benefit from diversity occurs in a study that looks at immigration and invention activity in the United States.[18] With its focus on patenting activity, the study demonstrates that immigrants to the United States directly contribute to the United States economy. In addition, immigrant patenting activity also had the indirect effect of making native-born Americans more productive (e.g., filing more patents). Certainly, this suggests that innovation is not a zero-sum game.

Sometimes the benefits of diversity are most visible at the team level in our day-to-day work. A study found that leaders who give diverse voices equal airtime are twice as likely to unleash value-driving insights.[19] Further, employees in a "speak up" culture are 3.5 times more likely to contribute to their full innovative potential. Unlocking innovative ideas makes things better for minority and majority populations as they individually and collectively reach their full innovative potential. Where are the losers in this equation?

Perhaps most reflective of reality, the authors within this same research evaluate companies with two-dimensional (2-D) diversity.[20] 2-D diversity includes things we traditionally think of in the space (e.g., ethnic, gender, orientation, religious affiliation, etc.), as well as professional diversity (e.g., doctors working with pharmacists, biologists with chemists, engineers with artists, etc.). The research found that companies with higher 2-D diversity were 45 percent more likely to report market share growth and 70 percent more likely to report capturing a new market. The consequences went both ways. Companies without 2-D diversity in their leadership resulted in women being 20 percent less likely to win endorsement of their ideas, people of color being 24 percent less likely, and members of the LGBTQ community being 21 percent less likely. Simply put, bringing diverse perspectives into the room matters. However, you cannot just throw diverse people together, walk out of the room, and expect magic to happen.

There Are Consequences If We Do This Incorrectly

A study reviewed the effectiveness of professionally diverse healthcare teams (e.g., doctors, nurses, etc.) at developing innovative clinical approaches to solve complex healthcare problems.[21] They found evidence that collaboration among this diverse group created conflict and was frequently unsuccessful. Additional studies found that heterogeneous groups experience communication problems, more conflict, and higher turnover rates.[22] This may be intuitive. If we work with people who look like us and think like us, there are clear efficiency gains. The idea is that we communicate better with colleagues who look and think like we do. These findings should surprise no one. Yet how can diversity drive innovation and performance and do the opposite at the same time?

Studies of the banking sector provide an important clue.[23] A study of banks found that racial diversity drives performance in earlier stages of development but resulted in economic performance losses in later stages. The study continues that racial diversity resulted in higher returns on equity when firms were in growth stages, but that benefit flipped when banks were downsizing. In other words, when banks want to grow and innovate, then racial diversity helps. When a bank's strategy was in trouble and they needed to make cuts and drive efficiency, having people who could communicate really well with each other mattered. This is the critical nuance. If you want innovation, then you need diversity. If you want to downsize, homogeny helps. If you want to position yourself so that you don't have to downsize, our view is diversity is the path to success.

A Path Forward

The research provides important clues around associations between diversity, innovation, and performance. The research certainly contradicts common narratives in the popular press. The stories in this book provide both the rationale and the missing details needed to explore this innovation frontier.

ACKNOWLEDGMENTS

This book has been a passion for the two of us for several years. It began during the turmoil of a pandemic and much social unrest. It also traversed a fast-evolving political dynamic over a tumultuous period. We come from contrasting backgrounds and views but always come together in a desire to maximize the value of all people here in the United States and the rest of the world. Together, we enjoy the celebration and admiration of innovation from the many cultures we have experienced in our own, very different, global journeys.

This book would be nothing without the insights from the many interviews we performed over the last few years. We hope you have enjoyed these very unique and personal stories. Our friend Keith Houlihan was present for all of them and was instrumental in helping us capture these stories and working with us to craft the emerging themes.

The writing of the book was supported by our three contributing authors. Maya Fitzgerald, a fresh-faced PharmD student, was our early research fellow. She, too, has a unique cultural background and passion for this subject, and her research was, in many ways, the early foundation for the text. Ashlie Thomas is a friend, colleague, and in many ways a personification of the potential represented in the book. We admire her passion and positivity. This book would not have happened without her commitment. Reuben Blackwell is a man of the civil rights movement and a constant advocate for his community in Rocky Mount, North Carolina. His sage advice to us on the book was also vital.

As first-time authors, we were keen to find the right publishing house. Rohit Bhargava and his Ideapress colleagues are a very different publisher with a passion for the subject matter represented here. We were so impressed by the work they completed for our collaborator Elliott Parker (CEO of High Alpha Innovation) on his book that we had to garner an introduction to Rohit and his team. Thanks to you all.

It would be remiss if we did not use this point to thank our research assistants, Aliyah Cruz and Stephania Zhang as well as our friends and colleagues at the Eshelman School of Pharmacy at UNC-Chapel Hill and, in particular, the Eshelman Innovation team. Your passion for innovation from all was an inspiration for this book. Special thanks to the leadership of Dr. Angela Kashuba as dean of the school.

We would like to thank our families. We have dedicated a great deal of time to this book, and we appreciate your love and support throughout. We hope this book makes this world a little better for each of you.

Finally, in this book we represent the dedication and application of the African American community to innovation in their own unique way. We must thank this community directly: We are incredibly grateful for your willingness to embrace the ideas represented in the text. The community exemplifies what is possible for all of humanity if we are willing to unlock the potential of all communities, Black and White. We hope this book contributes to an aspiration that we can all do better to value innovation for the benefit of all.

ENDNOTES

INTRODUCTION

1. World Economic Forum. "The Top 100 Companies of the World: The US vs. Everyone Else." July 27, 2021. https://www.weforum.org/stories/2021/07/top-100-companies-usa-china-money-capital-market/#:~:text=The%20world's%20top%20100%20companies,cap%20value%20of%20the%20list.
2. Startup Ranking. "Countries." Accessed April 26, 2025. https://www.startupranking.com/countries.
3. Enginsoy, Sengul. "Top Unicorn Cities & Countries in 2023." StartupBlink. December 13, 2023. https://www.startupblink.com/blog/top-unicorn-cities-and-countries/#:~:text=In%20total%2C%20there%20are%2051,worldwide%20with%20a%20PRO%20account.
4. Prosperity Institute. "The Legatum Prosperity Index™ 2023." Accessed April 16, 2025. https://index.prosperity.com/rankings.
5. NYU Langone Health. "Large Life Expectancy Gaps in US Cities Linked to Racial & Ethnic Segregation by Neighborhood." June 5, 2019. https://nyulangone.org/news/large-life-expectancy-gaps-us-cities-linked-racial-ethnic-segregation-neighborhood.
6. Waidmann, Timothy, Kristen Brown, Karishma Furtado, and Vincent Pancini. "State Variation in Black and White Life Expectancy and Evolving Disparities." Urban Institute. Last modified January 30, 2025. https://www.urban.org/sites/default/files/2025-01/corrected_State%20Variation_in_Black_and_White_Life_Expectancy_and_Evolving_Disparities.pdf.
7. Cooper, David, and Jessica Schieder. "By the Numbers: Income and Poverty, 2016." Economic Policy Institute. September 12, 2017. https://www.epi.org/

blog/by-the-numbers-income-and-poverty-2016/#:~:text=Median%20household%20income%20for%20white%2C%20non%2DHispanic%20households.

CHAPTER 1

1. Madam C. J. Walker. "Home Page." Accessed April 16, 2025. https://madamcjwalker.com.
2. Clark, Alexis. "Tulsa's 'Black Wall Street' Flourished as a Self-Contained Hub in Early 1900s." History. Last modified March 5, 2025. https://www.history.com/articles/black-wall-street-tulsa-race-massacre.
3. The Editors of Encyclopaedia Britannica. "Black Wall Street." Encyclopaedia Britannica. February 15, 2025. https://www.britannica.com/place/Black-Wall-Street.
4. Go Greenwood. "The People." Accessed April 16, 2025. https://gogreenwood.com/history/thepeople/.
5. Tulsa Historical Society and Museum. "1921 Tulsa Race Massacre." Accessed April 16, 2025. https://www.tulsahistory.org/exhibit/1921-tulsa-race-massacre/#:~:text=Although%20the%20exact%20total%20can,county%2C%20state%2C%20or%20federal.
6. Prieto, Dr. Leon, and Dr. Simone Phipps. "The Four Cardinal Points of Entrepreneurship: Lessons from Charles Clinton Spaulding." Thinkers50. Accessed April 16, 2025. https://thinkers50.com/blog/the-four-cardinal-points-of-entrepreneurship-lessons-from-charles-clinton-spaulding/.
7. Howell, Elizabeth A. "Reducing Disparities in Severe Maternal Morbidity and Mortality." *Clinical Obstetrics and Gynecology* vol. 61, no. 2 (June 2018): 387–399. https://doi.org/10.1097/GRF.0000000000000349.
8. Perry, Andre M., and Carl Romer. "To Expand the Economy, Invest in Black Businesses." Brookings. December 31, 2020. https://www.brookings.edu/articles/to-expand-the-economy-invest-in-black-businesses/.
9. Unnikrishnan, Shalini, and Cherie Blair. "Want to Boost the Global Economy by $5 Trillion? Support Women as Entrepreneurs." BCG. July 30, 2019. https://www.bcg.com/publications/2019/boost-global-economy-5-trillion-dollar-support-women-entrepreneurs.

CHAPTER 2

1. Legal Defense Fund. "Black Farmers FAQ." NAACP Legal Defense and Educational Fund. Accessed April 16, 2025. https://www.naacpldf.org/case-issue/black-farmers-faq/#:~:text=Today%2C%20the%20U.S.%20Department%20of%20Agriculture%20estimates,of%20farmland%20owned%20by%20their%20white%20counterparts.
2. Price, Austin. "Reversing the Trend of Black Land Loss." Berkeley Food Institute. April 28, 2023. https://food.berkeley.edu/q-and-a/reversing-the-trend-

of-black-land-loss/#:~:text=close%20to%20impossible.-,From%201992%20 to%202002%2C%2094%20percent%20of%20Black%20farmers%20lost, farmland%20ownership%20in%20the%20country.

3   Forbes, Yasmin. *United States History II: Module 7: The Jazz Age (1919–1929): The Great Migration.* Lumen Learning. Accessed April 17, 2025. https://courses.lumenlearning.com/wm-ushistory2/chapter/the-great-migration/.

4   Hazirjian, Lisa Gayle. "Combating NEED: Urban Conflict and the Transformations of the War on Poverty and the African American Freedom Struggle in Rocky Mount, North Carolina." *Journal of Urban History* vol. 34, no. 4 (March 2008): 639–664. https://doi.org/10.1177/0096144207312884.

5   Hill, Michael. "Martin Luther King, Jr.: Speech in Rocky Mount, NC, November 1962." NC Pedia. Last modified July 2023. https://www.ncpedia.org/martin-luther-king-jr-speech-rocky-mount-1962.

6   King, Dr. Martin Luther, Jr. "MLK's Forgotten Call for Economic Justice." *The Nation.* March 14, 1966. https://www.thenation.com/article/economy/last-steep-ascent/.

7   Interview with Reuben Blackwell, online, October 26, 2021.

8   Forbes. "Best Small Places for Business and Careers 2019: Rocky Mount, NC." Accessed April 17, 2025. https://www.forbes.com/places/nc/rocky-mount/.

9   Frey, William H. "A 'New Great Migration' Is Bringing Black Americans Back to the South." Brookings. September 12, 2022. https://www.brookings.edu/articles/a-new-great-migration-is-bringing-black-americans-back-to-the-south/.

CHAPTER 3

1   Green, Erica L. "Why Students Are Choosing HBCUs: '4 Years Being Seen as Family.'" *The New York Times.* Last modified June 22, 2023. https://www.nytimes.com/2022/06/11/us/hbcu-enrollment-black-students.html#.

2   Green, Erica L. "Why Students Are Choosing HBCUs: '4 Years Being Seen as Family.'" *The New York Times.* Last modified June 22, 2023. https://www.nytimes.com/2022/06/11/us/hbcu-enrollment-black-students.html#.

3   Lumpkin, Lauren, Nick Anderson, and Danielle Douglas-Gabriel. "Amid Nationwide Enrollment Drops, Some HBCUs Are Growing. So Are Threats." *The Washington Post.* Last modified February 16, 2022. https://www.washingtonpost.com/education/2022/02/11/hbcu-enrollment-growth-bomb-threats/.

4   Legal Defense Fund. "Nikole Hannah-Jones Issues Statement on Decision to Decline Tenure Offer at University of North Carolina–Chapel Hill and to Accept Knight Chair Appointment at Howard University." July 6, 2021. https://www.naacpldf.org/press-release/nikole-hannah-jones-issues-statement-on-decision-to-decline-tenure-offer-at-university-of-north-carolina-chapel-hill-and-

to-accept-knight-chair-appointment-at-howard-university/#:~:text=And%20
I%20have%20decided%20that,for%20those%20who%20once%20were.
5   Interview with Bernard Bell, online, August 11, 2022.
6   Interview with Nehemiah Stewart, online, July 21, 2022.
7   Interview with Joel Wiggins, online, July 25, 2022.

CHAPTER 4

1   International Boxing Hall of Fame. "Max Schmeling." Accessed April 17, 2025. http://www.ibhof.com/pages/about/inductees/modern/schmeling.html#:~:-text=PERHAPS%20BEST%20remembered%20in%20the,Hitler%20to%20demonstrate%20Aryan%20supremacy.
2   Lapointe, Joe. "The Championship Fight That Went Beyond Boxing." *The New York Times*. June 19, 1988. https://www.nytimes.com/1988/06/19/sports/the-championship-fight-that-went-beyond-boxing.html.
3   Dubner, Stephen J., host. "Episode 480: How Much Does Discrimination Hurt the Economy?" *Freakonomics Economy* (podcast). October 27, 2021. Accessed April 17, 2025. https://freakonomics.com/podcast/how-much-does-discrimination-hurt-the-economy/.
4   Murray, Jim. "The Loser Was Big Winner." *Los Angeles Times*. July 18, 1991. https://www.latimes.com/archives/la-xpm-1991-07-18-sp-3409-story.html.
5   Sports Business Journal. "Shaq Gets Behind New Ad Agency Focused on Diversity." March 1, 2021. https://www.sportsbusinessjournal.com/SB-Blogs/SBJ-Unpacks/2021/03/02/SPAC/.
6   Interview with Karen LeVert, online, September 26, 2022.
7   Pedersen-Pietersen, Laura. "An Online Matchmaker of Athletes and Schools." *The New York Times*. February 20, 2020. https://archive.nytimes.com/www.nytimes.com/library/financial/personal/022000personal-callings.html.
8   Major, Derek. "Black Equity: Robert L. Johnson Created the Most Black Millionaires in US History After Selling BET." Yahoo! Finance. October 17, 2022. https://finance.yahoo.com/news/black-equity-robert-l-johnson-165820045.html?guccounter=1.

CHAPTER 5

1   Ashworth, William B., Jr. "Scientist of the Day: George Washington Carver." Linda Hall Library. Accessed April 17, 2025. https://www.lindahall.org/about/news/scientist-of-the-day/george-washington-carver/.
2   Interview with Ashlie Thomas, online, November 3, 2022.
3   Gormley, Brian. "Food-as-Medicine' Startups Draw Venture Capital." *The Wall Street Journal*. October 6, 2022. https://www.wsj.com/articles/food-as-medicine-startups-draw-venture-capital-11665050402.

ENDNOTES

4 Somaiya, Mihir, and Uday Suresh. "Q3 2022 Digital Health Funding: The Market Isn't the Same as It Was." Rock Health. October 3, 2022. https://rockhealth.com/insights/q3-2022-digital-health-funding-the-market-isnt-the-same-as-it-was/.

5 KFF. "Disparities in Health and Health Care Among Black People." February 24, 2022. https://www.kff.org/infographic/disparities-in-health-and-health-care-among-black-people/.

6 World Health Organization. "Surgical Site Infection." Accessed April 17, 2025. https://www.who.int/teams/integrated-health-services/infection-prevention-control/surgical-site-infection#:~:text=Surgical%20site%20infections%20are%20caused,to%20care%20for%20their%20babies.

7 Fortune Business Insights. "Surgical Sutures Market Size, Share & Industry Analysis, by Product Type (Absorbable and Non-Absorbable), by Form (Natural and Synthetic), by Application (Gynecology, Cardiology, Orthopedics, General Surgery, and Others), by End-user (Hospitals & ASCs and Specialty Clinics), and Regional Forecast, 2025–2032." March 31, 2025. https://www.fortunebusinessinsights.com/industry-reports/surgical-sutures-market-100660.

8 Twin Cities Business. "RetraceHealth Ceasing Operations." April 19, 2017. https://tcbmag.com/retracehealth-ceasing-operations/.

9 J Lab Admin. "The Anomaly of Ellington West, CEO of Sonavi Labs: Being Raised by a Black Man Who Changed the World as We Know It." Johnson & Johnson. February 23, 2021. https://jnjinnovation.com/news/blog-post/the-anomaly-of-ellington-west-ceo-of-sonavi-labs-being-raised-by-a-black-man-who-changed-the-world-as-we-know-it.

10 Landi, Heather. "Incredible Health Vaults to Unicorn Status, Scores $80M to Grow Its Healthcare Job Matching Service." Fierce Healthcare. August 19, 2022. https://www.fiercehealthcare.com/health-tech/incredible-health-vaults-unicorn-status-scores-80m-grow-its-healthcare-job-matching.

11 Players Health. "Players Health Raises $28 Million in Latest Funding Round to Continue Mission of Protecting Youth Athletes." March 23, 2022. https://www.playershealth.com/resources/players-health-raises-28-million-latest-funding-round-continue.

12 Evans, Farrell. "How a Bigoted Investor Inspired This Founder to Embrace Himself and His Community." *Inc.* April 11, 2024. https://www.inc.com/farrell-evans/how-bigoted-investor-inspired-this-founder-embrace-himself-community.html.

13 Petruzzi, D. "Revenue of the Beauty & Personal Care Market in the United States from 2020 to 2030." Statista. February 11, 2025. https://www.statista.com/forecasts/1448062/revenue-beauty-personal-care-beauty-personal-care-market-united-states.

14 Wilhelm, Alex. "Rebundle Raises $1.4M for Plant-Based Hair Extensions." TechCrunch. January 17, 2022. https://techcrunch.com/2022/01/17/rebundle-raises-1-4m-for-plant-based-hair-extensions/.
15 Upland. "Fenty Beauty: Leveraging Social Media to Build Community." Accessed April 17, 2025. https://go-upland.com/fenty-beauty-leveraging-social-media-to-build-community/#:~:text=Rihanna's%20Fenty%20Beauty%20is%20a,Stunna%20Lip%20Paint%20in%20red.

CHAPTER 6

1 Tennessee Department of Economic and Community Development. "Healthcare and Life Sciences." Accessed April 17, 2025. https://tnecd.com/industries/healthcare-and-life-sciences/#:~:text=In%20Middle%20Tennessee%20alone%2C%20the,the%20Nashville%20Health%20Care%20Council.
2 Farmer, Blake. "Nashville's Health Care Companies Were Pushed to Confront Racism. Now They're Investing in Black Startups." WPLN News. January 31, 2022. https://wpln.org/post/nashvilles-health-care-companies-were-pushed-to-confront-racism-now-theyre-investing-in-black-startups/.
3 Interview with Marcus Whitney, February 16, 2023.
4 Columbia Business School—The Eugene Lang Entrepreneurship Center. "Why Don't More Minorities Launch VC-Backed Businesses? Plus 4 Ways VCs Can Help." *Forbes*. July 22, 2021. https://www.forbes.com/sites/columbiabusinessschool/2021/07/22/why-dont-more-minorities-launch-vc-backed-businesses-plus-4-ways-vcs-can-help/?sh=7ec5a7094ed2.
5 Bek, Nate. "A Trio of Founders Offer Lessons on 'Fundraising While Black' in Techstars Panel Discussion." GeekWire. June 16, 2022. https://www.geekwire.com/2022/a-trio-of-founders-offer-lessons-on-fundraising-while-black-in-techstars-panel-discussion/.
6 Suazo, Ritza. "Why Venture Studio Startups Have Higher Long-Term Success Rates." Bundl. Accessed April 17, 2025. https://www.bundl.com/articles/why-venture-studio-startups-have-higher-long-term-success-rates.
7 Interview with Renard Charity, online, January 24, 2023.

CHAPTER 7

1 Companies Marketcap. "Largest Pharma Companies by Market Cap." Accessed April 17, 2025. https://companiesmarketcap.com/pharmaceuticals/largest-pharmaceutical-companies-by-market-cap/#google_vignette.
2 Interview with Sue Mahony, December 16, 2022.
3 Huang, Jess, Alexis Krivkovich, Irina Starikova, Lareina Yee, and Delia Zanoschi. "Women in the Workplace 2019." McKinsey & Company. October 2019. https://www.mckinsey.com/~/media/McKinsey/Featured%20Insights/Gender%20Equality/Women%20in%20the%20Workplace%202019/Women-

in-the-workplace-2019.pdf.

4 Purmal, Kate, Lee Epting, and Joshua Isaac Smith. *Composure: The Art of Executive Presence.* Amplify Publishing, 2021.

5 Gishuru, Kabi. "Creating More Access for Black Students into the Tech World." Netflix. October 22, 2020. https://about.netflix.com/en/news/creating-more-access-for-black-students-in-tech.

6 Fidelity. "Fidelity's 2023 Diversity and Inclusion Report: Associate Population Continued to Grow Across All Ethnic and Gender Groups." Accessed April 18, 2025. https://newsroom.fidelity.com/pressreleases/fidelity-s-2023-diversity-and-inclusion-report--associate-population-continued-to-grow-across-all-et/s/7e773fa9-a138-40b2-a272-d402451c347a.

CHAPTER 8

1 Hodgkin, Douglas I. "History of Lewiston." Accessed April 18, 2025. https://www.lewistonmaine.gov/421/History-of-Lewiston.

2 Washuk, Bonnie. "Lower Lisbon Street Filling with Somali businesses." *Sun Journal.* August 29, 2010. https://www.sunjournal.com/2010/08/29/lower-lisbon-street-filling-somali-businesses/.

3 Anderson, Cynthia. "Refugees Poured into My State. Here's How It Changed Me." *The Christian Science Monitor.* Last modified October 18, 2019. https://www.csmonitor.com/USA/2019/1028/Refugees-poured-into-my-state.-Here-s-how-it-changed-me.

4 McCandlish, Laura. "Somali Refugees Build a Future as Farmers—in Maine." The World. November 29, 2013. https://theworld.org/stories/2013/11/29/somali-refugees-taking-root-farmers-maine.

5 Minnesota Department of Human Services. "Salman Elmi." Last modified June 9, 2022. https://mn.gov/dhs/outstanding-refugees/profiles/salman-elmi/.

6 Shaw, Lily. "Startup Showcase: Entrepreneur Meets Restaurateur with New App." June 30, 2018. https://www.twincities.com/2018/06/30/startup-showcase-entrepreneur-meets-restaurateur-with-new-app/.

7 Duggan, J.D. "Minneapolis Startup Tavolo Joins Farm to Fork Accelerator from Ecolab, Techstars." Minneinno. Last modified August 10, 2023. https://www.bizjournals.com/twincities/inno/stories/news/2023/08/10/tavolo-first-local-farm-to-fork.html.

8 Gerezgiher, Feven. "New Partnership Offers Work-Safe Hijabs for Amazon Employees in Brooklyn Park." MPR News. August 17, 2023. https://www.mprnews.org/story/2023/08/17/new-partnership-offers-worksafe-hijabs-for-amazon-employees-in-brooklyn-park.

9   Interview with Shuchin Shukla, September 21, 2023.
10 Mental Health America. "Evidence for Peer Support." May 2019. https://mhanational.org/wp-content/uploads/2025/02/Evidence-Peer-Support-May-2019.pdf.
11 Videka, Lynn, Jodie Neale, Cory Page, et al. *National Analysis of Peer Support Providers: Practice Settings, Requirements, Roles, and Reimbursement.* UM Behavioral Health Workforce Research Center: Health Workforce Technical Assistance Center, 2019. https://www.healthworkforceta.org/research-alerts/national-analysis-of-peer-support-providers-practice-settings-requirements-roles-and-reimbursement/.
12 Mental Health America. "Evidence for Peer Support." May 2019. https://mhanational.org/wp-content/uploads/2025/02/Evidence-Peer-Support-May-2019.pdf.
13 Journal Record Staff. "Oklahoma Entrepreneurs Launch Digital Bank Totem." *The Journal Record*. August 17, 2022. https://journalrecord.com/2022/08/17/oklahoma-entrepreneurs-launch-digital-bank-totem/.
14 Interview with Marcus Whitney, February 16, 2023.
15 Dixon-Fyle, Sundiatu, Kevin Dolan, Dame Vivian Hunt, and Sara Prince. *Diversity Wins: How Inclusion Matters.* McKinsey & Company, 2020. https://www.mckinsey.com/featured-insights/diversity-and-inclusion/diversity-wins-how-inclusion-matters.
16 Lorenzo, Rocío, Nicole Voigt, Miki Tsusaka, Matt Krentz, and Katie Abouzahr. "How Diverse Leadership Teams Boost Innovation." BCG. 2018. https://www.bcg.com/publications/2018/how-diverse-leadership-teams-boost-innovation.
17 Freeman, Richard B., and Wei Huang. "Collaborating with People Like Me: Ethnic Coauthorship within the United States." *Journal of Labor Economics* vol. 33, no. 3 (July 2015): 289–318. https://doi.org/10.1086/678973.
18 Bernstein, Shai, Rebecca Diamond, Abhisit Jiranaphawiboon, Timothy McQuade, and Beatriz Pousada. "The Contribution of High-Skilled Immigrants to Innovation in the United States." *National Bureau of Economic Research* (December 2022). https://www.nber.org/papers/w30797.
19 Hewlett, Sylvia Ann, Melinda Marshall, and Laura Sherbin. "How Diversity Can Drive Innovation." *Harvard Business Review*. December 2013. https://hbr.org/2013/12/how-diversity-can-drive-innovation.
20 Hewlett, Sylvia Ann, Melinda Marshall, and Laura Sherbin. "How Diversity Can Drive Innovation." *Harvard Business Review*. December 2013. https://hbr.org/2013/12/how-diversity-can-drive-innovation.
21 Mitchell, Rebecca, and Brendan Boyle. "Professional Diversity, Identity Salience, and Team Innovation: The Moderating Role of Openmindedness

Norms." *Journal of Organizational Behavior* vol. 36, no. 6 (August 2015): 873–894. https://www.jstor.org/stable/26611018.

22 Chatman, Jennifer A., Barsade, Sigal, and Margaret A. Neale. "Being Different Yet Feeling Similar: The Influence of Demographic Composition and Organizational Culture on Work Processes and Outcomes." *Administrative Science Quarterly* vol. 43, no. 4 (December 1998): 749–780. http://dx.doi.org/10.2307/2393615.

23 Richard, Orlando C., and David Ford. "Exploring the Performance Effects of Visible Attribute Diversity: The Moderating Role of Span of Control and Organizational Life Cycle." *The International Journal of Human Resource Management* vol. 17, no. 12 (January 2007): 2091–2109. http://dx.doi.org/10.1080/09585190601000246.

INDEX

A

Abuzeid, Iman, 129
Abyssinian Baptist Church, 54–55
accelerating transformative change.
 See transformative change
Aderinkomi, Thompson, 127–128
Adidas, 100
Admiral Capital Group, 101
Affordable Care Act (2010), 126
African American entrepreneurs. See
 Black entrepreneurialism
 and innovation
African American Journey, The
 (Eli Lilly), 160–164, 169
Ahmed, Hussein, 177
Alexander, Will, 192–193
Ali, Muhammad, 98
Aliweyd, Asad, 179
All Stars Helping Kids, 145
Amazon, 178, 186
American Tobacco Company, 45
American Underground, 34–35
Amgen, 166–167
Andreessen, Marc, 116
AnnexTech Partners, 35

Appalachia opioid crisis, 181–187
Apple, 124
Armstrong, Louis, 52
Associated Press, 95
Aston University, 10, 165, 166
athletics. See sports
Atlanta, Georgia, 62–63
Autodesk, 106–107

B

Bamforth, John, 9–10, 17, 45, 143, 157,
 164–165
Bandwagon, 130–132
banks
 history of Black entrepreneurialism with, 23–26, 29
 loans and mortgages from, 22,
  24–26, 27, 40, 69
Basie, Count, 52
Battelle Memorial Institute, 34
BCG (Boston Consulting Group),
 40, 155
Beans, Fred, 87–88
Beats Electronics, 124
beauty industry, 18–22, 132–133
Bell, Bernard, 67–75, 78–79

211

Bell Labs, 128
Bernstein, Jim, 58–59
Berry, Simon, 27
BET (Black Entertainment Television), 74, 101, 111–112
Better Homes and Gardens, 122
Bitly, 150
Black Belt, 47–50, 62–63, 65
Black entrepreneurialism and innovation
   authors' experiences and perceptions of, 12–13, 16
   enclaves backing (*see* education enclaves; enclaves)
   expansion beyond (*see* innovation zone expansion)
   goals of, 5–6
   hidden history of (*see* history of Black entrepreneurialism and innovation)
   impacts of, generally, 5
   ownership by (*see* ownership)
   racial disparities impacting (*see* racial disparities)
   stimulation of (*see* stimulation of innovation)
   support for (*see* support for innovation)
   transformative change through (*see* transformative change)
   unique lenses on market in (*see* unique lenses)
Black Entrepreneurial Network, 57
Black History Month, 163
Black Lives Matter, 136
Black Wall Streets, 22–36, 43, 62, 189
Blackwell, Reuben, 45–46, 55–61, 177
Boots Group, 166

Boston Consulting Group (BCG), 40, 155
Braddock, James, 95
Branson, Richard, 174
Breedlove, Sarah (Madam C. J. Walker), 17–22, 41, 62, 132
Brigham Young University, 11
Bristol Myers Squibb, 167
Bronx, New York, 180–181
Brookings Institute, 40
Budweiser, 32
Buker, Amber, 188
Burks, Tyrre, 129–130

C

Cabell, Samuel, 54
Caesars Palace, 95
Cambridge University, 165
Canadian Football League, 129
Carver, George Washington, 115–116
Cathedral Innovation Group, 34
Celebrate Family, 89
Center for Creative Leadership, 105
Center of Excellence in Entrepreneurship and Innovation, 80
Chance, Richard, 188
Change and Rotation, 89
Charity, Renard, 154–155
Charlotte Hornets (formerly Bobcats), 101
Chauvin, Derek, 135
Cherokee Nation, 188
Chevrolet, 100
Choctaw Nation, 188
churches, 23, 54–55, 61–62, 76, 98
Cisco Systems, 35
Citizen Schools, 145
Clark Atlanta University, 172
Clemson University, 130

Clinton, Hillary, 74
Club Med, 106
Coca-Cola, 97, 100
CODE2040, 35
Cole, Aisha "Pinky," 171–175
Collins, Susan, 177
Colored June German, 52
Coltrane, John, 52
community support
    enclaves as (*see* enclaves)
    for founders, 148
    innovation zone expansion benefitting, 175–189
    ownership and contributions to, 89–90
    trust building and, 153–155
    unique lenses for, 120–123, 128–129, 131–132
companies. *See also by name*
    community support through, 89–90
    corporate social responsibility of, 30
    diversity in, 6, 158–170, 194–195
    educational outreach by, 71
    enclaves in Black-led, 74–75
    ownership of (*see* ownership)
    startup (*see* startups)
    stimulation of innovation by, 8, 157–170
    US market value of, 3
Composure: The Art of Executive Presence (Purmal), 168
Compton, California, 124
Compton Vegan, 123–124
Converse, 100
C.O.R.E. Services, 32
corporate social responsibility, 30

cosmetics. *See* beauty industry
cotton, 46, 47, 50–51, 56
COVID-19 pandemic
    educational effects of, 67, 79, 90
    healthcare and, 126, 128, 140, 181
    racial disparities in effects of, 126
    Stewart's business changes in, 79
    transformative change from, 140
Crowell, Mark, 33
customer journey mapping, 159

D

Daily Harvest, 39
Declaration of Independence, 13–14
DEI. *See* diversity, equity, and inclusion
Detroit Pistons, 101
Dill, David, 191–193
Discovery Channel, 73–74
diversity, equity, and inclusion
    challenges of, 196–197
    Eli Lilly analyzing and promoting, 158–170
    innovation facilitated by, 6
    innovation zone expansion with, 174, 175–179, 188–189, 194–197
    in leadership, 137–138, 154, 159, 169–170, 195
    ownership backing, 102, 109–110
    professional, 196
    research on, 194–197
    sustainability of, 5
    two-dimensional, 196
    unique lenses through, 113–114, 117, 123, 128–129, 133
    in venture capital, 146–147
    in venture studio model, 152

Dogwood Health Trust, 182
Douglas Block, 51, 60
Dr. Dre, 124
Du Bois, W. E. B., 30
Duke, 45
Duke University, 33, 107–108
Durham, North Carolina, 29–30, 34
Durrah, Lemel, 123–124

E

Eastern Michigan University, 104
economy. *See also* socioeconomic status
    Black Wall Streets and, 22–36, 43, 62, 189
    community changes in, 175–179
    companies in (*see* companies)
    diversity value to, 194–196
    innovation for growth of, 4–5, 13, 42
    loans and mortgages in, 22, 24–26, 27, 40, 69, 146
    loss from minority underrepresentation in, 4, 40–41
    venture capital in (*see* venture capital)
Edison, Thomas, 116
education enclaves, 65–91
    Bell's story and, 67–75, 78–79
    charter schools as, 145
    diversity value in, 195
    entrepreneurial experience beyond, 80–91
    HBCUs as, 54, 65–67, 79–81, 91, 161 (*see also* historically Black colleges and universities)
    innovation zone expansion support via, 179–180
    integration and, 70, 76
    Mahony's story on, 165–166
    mindset and, 71–74, 81–84, 87–91
    OIC as, 55–57
    ongoing benefits of, 75–80
    segregation and, 65–66, 104, 115
    Stewart's story and, 75–80
    students as assets in, 90–91
    Whitney's story and, 138
    Wiggins's story and, 80–91
Eli Lilly and Company, 157–170
    African American experiences working at, 160–164, 169
    Bamforth at, 10, 17, 157
    diversity analysis and promotion in, 158–170
    history of, 158
    innovation stimulation by, 8, 157–159, 162, 170
    Mahony's story and, 164–170
    women's experiences working at, 159–160, 162, 164, 167–170
Elmi, Salman, 178
Emergency Services Sector (ESS), 184, 187
Emerging Startup of the Year, 178
empowerment
    economic, 23
    enclaves supporting, 53
    ownership and, 14, 81–82, 94
    of unique lenses, 7
enclaves, 45–63
    Atlanta as, 62–63
    Bell's story of, 67–75
    Black Belt and, 47–50, 62–63
    Blackwell's story and, 45–46, 55–61
    churches and, 54–55, 61–62, 76
    of education (*see* education enclaves)
    Great Migration and, 49–50, 55, 63

healthcare access support in, 56, 57–60
history of entrepreneurial support in, 21, 33, 61
innovation zone expansion with, 174, 179–180, 191
OIC and, 55–61
overview of, 7
ownership support in, 56–57, 61–62, 93–94
psychological safety in, 168
racial disparities impacting, 48–53, 56–58, 60–61, 63
Rocky Mount as, 45–46, 50–53, 55–61, 63
shifting mindset in, 56–57
Sullivan's story and, 53–56, 57, 62
on television, 74–75
endorsements, celebrity, 99–102, 173
enslaved African Americans
  Carver's experience as, 115
  demographics of, 47–48
  emancipation of, 54, 61
  farming stigma from, 121–122
  post-emancipation status of, 22–23, 25–26, 41 (*see also* history of Black entrepreneurialism and innovation)
  in Rocky Mount, 50–51
entertainment
  Bell in, 73–75
  Black-focused, 63, 74–75, 101, 111–112
  ownership path from, 110–112
  sports as (*see* sports)
  unique lenses on, 129–132
entrepreneurialism. *See* innovation and entrepreneurialism
Environmental Biotech, 106

Eshelman Innovation
  Bamforth at, 10, 45, 143, 157
  goals of, 121
  on opioid crisis, 181–182, 186
  strength-based focus of, 45
  Thomas at, 117, 121–122
  transformative change with, 143–144, 149, 151–155
  Zwahlen at, 11
ESPN, 111
ESS (Emergency Services Sector), 184, 187
Esusu, 38
Evans, Marlon, 144–149
ExactTarget, 149
expansion of innovation zone. *See* innovation zone expansion
Ezell, Tony, 160–164

F

Facebook, 131
farms, 48–49, 68, 116, 118–120, 177–178. *See also* gardening
Farm to Fork Accelerator, 178
Federal-Aid Highway Act (1956), 93–94
federally qualified health clinics (FQHCs), 60, 185
Feelix, 128
Fenty Beauty, 132–133
Fenway Sports Group, 102
Fidelity, 170
FIFA World Cup, 190
Fitzgerald, Ella, 52
Fletcher Spaght, 155
Florida A&M, 161
Floyd, George, 2, 11, 79, 135–136, 140, 146

Food, Nutrition, and Health Investor Coalition, 123
food and nutrition, 119–125, 152, 178
Forbes, 60
Ford, Henry, 116
Ford, Henry, II, 96–97
Ford Motor Company and dealerships, 85–89, 95, 96–97, 116
Foreman, George, 98–99
FQHCs (federally qualified health clinics), 60, 185
Francis Marion University, 120
Franklin, Aretha, 74
Freedman's Bank, 23, 26
Freedmen's Bureau, 23, 66
Frog Town neighborhood, 94
Fusion Coalition, 25–26

G

gardening, 120–123, 124. *See also* farms
Gatorade, 100
Gatto, Vic, 140
General Electric, 116
George Foreman Grill, 99
George Mason University, 11
GI Bill, 103
Global Startup Studio Network, 151
Goestenkors, Gail, 107–108
Golden LEAF Foundation, 57
Goldie, 186–187
Google, 34, 102, 131
Great Migration, 49–50, 55, 63, 95
Green Book, 52
Greenwood neighborhood, 27–29
Gro Intelligence, 125
GSVlabs, 146
Gurley, O. W., 27

H

Hagerty, Bill, 192–193
Hanes, 101
Hanna, Melissa, 38
Hannah-Jones, Nikole, 67
Harlem, New York, 22, 54–55, 172
Harris Teeter, 83
Harvard University, 131, 195
HBCUs. *See* historically Black colleges and universities
healthcare
  COVID-19 pandemic and, 126, 128, 140, 181
  diversity in, 196–197
  enclaves supporting access to, 56, 57–60
  food and nutrition in, 121–125, 178
  history of Black entrepreneurialism in, 38–39
  innovation zone expansion in, 178, 179–187
  opioid crisis and, 181–187
  pharmaceuticals in (*see* Eli Lilly and Company)
  racial disparities in, 3, 37–38, 57–58, 124, 126–127, 136–137, 180–181
  Thomas family issues of, 118–120
  unique lenses for changes in, 125–129
  Whitney driving transformative change in, 136–141
Health Stream, 139
Henderson, Lisa, 106–107
Henna & Hijabs, 178–179
HGTV (Home and Garden Television), 73
High Alpha Innovation, 149, 182

INDEX

historically Black colleges and universities (HBCUs). *See also specific schools by name*
    as education enclaves, 54, 65–67, 79–81, 91, 161
    HBCU Founders Initiative, 123, 144, 148–149, 151–152
    innovation acceleration models developed with, 143–144, 147–149
history of Black entrepreneurialism and innovation, 17–43
    Black Wall Streets in, 22–36, 43, 189
    Breedlove/Walker story in, 17–22, 41, 62, 132
    cascading impacts of success in, 19, 21, 25–26, 29–30, 34, 41–43
    conditions for success in, 41–42
    Greenwood neighborhood in, 27–29
    loss from oppression in, 28–29, 40–41
    Malone's story in, 19–20
    North Carolina Mutual Life Insurance Company in, 29–30, 34
    overview of, 7
    patents in, 32–33
    politics and, 25–26
    socioeconomic status and wealth in, 18, 22–23, 25–27, 36–37
    Speight family story in, 30–36, 43
    St. Luke's Penny Savings Bank in, 23–25
    venture capital in, 35–39, 43
    White supremacy effects on, 26, 27–28
    Williams's story in, 36–39, 43
Hitler, Adolf, 96, 97
Home and Garden Television (HGTV), 73
home ownership, 22, 26, 69, 93–94, 104, 117, 164
Howard University, 66–67
HP, 146
HUED, 39
Hughes, Harold, 130–132
Humana Foundation, 152, 154
Hurricane Katrina, 180
Hussein, Fatuma, 177

I

IBM, 71–72, 138
Ibrahim, Hilal, 178–179
Idealab, 149
"I Have a Dream" speeches (King), 53, 61
Impossible Burgers, 173
Impossible Foods, 39
imposter syndrome, 168, 170
Incredible Health, 129
Independent Order of St. Luke, 23–24
Ingram, John/Ingram Group, 193
innovation and entrepreneurialism
    authors' experiences and perceptions of, 11–13, 16
    deficit of, 2, 3–6
    definition of, 14
    expansion of zone for (*see* innovation zone expansion)
    goals of, 14–16
    by marginalized entrepreneurs (*see* Black entrepreneurialism and innovation; marginalized entrepreneurs; women)
    ownership and (*see* ownership)
    solutions to facilitating, 6–9

stimulation of (see stimulation of innovation)
support for (see enclaves; support for innovation; venture capital)
transformative change with (see transformative change)
unique lenses on market in (see unique lenses)
innovation zone expansion, 171–197
   for Appalachia opioid crisis, 181–187
   Cole's story and, 171–175
   diversity driving, 174, 175–179, 188–189, 194–197
   enclaves supporting, 174, 179–180, 191
   in Lewiston, Maine, 175–178
   in Minnesota, 178–179
   for Nashville SC, 190–194
   overview of, 8
   ownership and, 189, 192–193
   pitch for accepting, 189–194
   problems as opportunities for, 179–187, 189–190
   purpose driving, 175–179, 187, 189
   research on value of, 194–197
   resistance to, 176–177, 189
   scalability and, 174, 187
   Shukla's story and, 179–183, 186–187
   by Somali immigrants, 176–179
   unique lenses on market for, 174, 192
   venture capital for, 174, 191–194
Integrated Training Academy, 57
integration, educational, 70, 76
intellectual property, 32–33, 128, 195–196
International Development Bank, 144
Iowa State University, 115–116
Iroquois Confederacy, 47

J

James, LeBron, 102
Jay-Z, 110
JCPenney, 111
Jefferson, Thomas, 13–14
Jobs, Steve, 174
Johns Hopkins University, 58, 128
Johnson, Kristina, 107–108
Johnson, Magic, 99–100, 101–102, 110
Johnson, Robert L., 101, 111
Johnson, Robert Wood, 60
Johnson, Sheila, 110–112
Johnson, Vinnie, 101
Jones, Chris, 190–191
Jordan, Michael, 7, 76, 100–101, 110
Jumpstart Foundry, 136, 140, 193
Jumpstart Nova, 141, 190
Jumpstart Our Country, 140
June Germans, 52
Junior Achievement, 145
Juno Medical, 39

K

Kicking It, 112
King, Billie Jean, 107
King, Martin Luther, Jr., 53, 55, 61–62, 173
Kingmaker Program, 89–90
Knight, Phil, 99–100
Knowledge Is Power Program (KIPP), 145
Ku Klux Klan (KKK), 27–28, 49, 95

INDEX

L

Lacuna, 79
Lechleiter, John, 158, 163
Legatum Prosperity Index, 3
Legend, John, 74
LevelEdge, 107–108
Level the Playing Field, 79–80
LeVert, Karen, 103–110
LeVert Ventures, 109–110
Lewiston, Maine, 175–178
life expectancy, 3
Lifepoint Health, 191
Liggett, 51
Lilly, Eli (Colonel), 158. *See also* Eli Lilly and Company
loans and mortgages, 22, 24–26, 27, 40, 69, 146. *See also* venture capital
Locke, John, 13–14
Los Angeles Lakers, 99, 102
Louis, Joe, 95–98
Louis Vitton, 132
Lowe, Ken, 73
LVMH, 132

M

Madam C. J. Walker Theater, 17–18
Magic Johnson Enterprises, 102
Mahmee, 38
Mahony, Sue, 164–170
Major League Soccer, 190, 193
Malone, Annie, 19–20
Manly brothers, 25
marginalized entrepreneurs. *See also* Black entrepreneurialism and innovation; women
  applicability of Black experiences for, 12
  expansion to include (*see* innovation zone expansion)
  hidden history of (*see* history of Black entrepreneurialism and innovation)
  innovation constraints for, 2, 12–13
  support for (*see* enclaves; support for innovation; venture capital)
markets
  company value in, 3
  underserved or undervalued, 6, 7, 39, 113–114, 153
  unique lenses on (see unique lenses)
Market Salamander, 112
Mastercard, 102
Matter to a Million, 146
May, Ciara Imani, 132
McDonald's, 100
McGhee, Heather, 40
McGonigal, Mrs., 76
McKinsey, 159, 168, 194–195
Medicaid, 58, 126, 179, 185, 186
Meharry Medical College, 137
Meineke, 99
Menker, Sara, 125
Merchants National Bank of Richmond, 24
Microsoft, 147
Miller, Thomas, 25
Miller Brewing Company, 32
mindset or mental attitude. *See also* perceptions
  education enclaves and, 71–74, 81–84, 87–91
  imposter syndrome affecting, 168, 170

219

for ownership, 81–84, 87–91
psychological safety in enclaves affecting, 168
racial disparities and, 56–57, 71–74, 81–82, 161–162
shifting, 56–57
survival, 170
for transformative change, 139, 148, 153, 155
unique lenses and, 122
Minnesota, immigrants in, 178–179
Mocha Gardener, The, 120
Moderna, 150
Morgan Stanley, 125, 155
Morgan State University, 66
Morrill Act (1862/1890), 65
mortgages. *See* loans and mortgages
Mountain Area Health Education Center, 182
Musk, Elon, 116

N

NASA, 33, 128
Nashville Health Care Fellows, 136
Nashville Health Care Leadership Council, 136–137, 140–141
Nashville Metros, 190
Nashville SC (formerly Nashville FC), 190–194
National Association for the Advancement of Colored People (NAACP), 22
National Basketball Association, 99–102
National Premier Soccer League, 190
National Rural Health Association, 59
Nationwide Insurance, 104–105
Netflix, 170

New American Development Center, 179
Nex Cubed, 123, 144, 146–149, 151–152
Nice Healthcare, 127–128, 129
Nike, 99–100, 107
Noom, 38–39
Nordstrom, 178
North Carolina Agricultural and Technical State University
   Bell's father at, 69
   enrollment at, 66–67
   Eshelman Innovation and, 143–144, 149, 152, 154
   Speight and, 31–33
   Wiggins at, 80–81, 83–85, 90–91
North Carolina Department of Health and Human Services, 56
North Carolina Mutual Life Insurance Company, 29–30, 34
North Carolina Office of Rural Health, 59
NWA, 124

O

Oak Ridge National Laboratory, 34
Obama, Barack and administration, 74–75, 108
Ohanian, Alexis, 37
Ohio State University, 108
O'Neal, Shaquille, 102
Operation Breadbasket, 55
opioid crisis, 181–187
Opportunities Industrialization Centers of America (OIC), 55–61
Orwell, George, 9
ownership, 93–112
   athletics as path to, 98–102, 112, 192–193

INDEX

community support through, 89–90
empowerment and, 14, 81–82, 94
enclaves supporting opportunities for, 56–57, 61–62, 93–94
entertainment as path to, 110–112
entrepreneurialism creating opportunities for, 87, 105–110
exposure to potential for, 103
of farms, 48–49, 68, 118–119
Foreman's story on, 98–99
history of, 19–22, 25, 26–27, 29–32
of homes, 22, 26, 69, 93–94, 104, 117, 164
innovation zone expansion and, 189, 192–193
James's story on, 102
Magic Johnson's story on, 99–100, 101–102
Sheila Johnson's story on, 110–112
Vinnie Johnson's story on, 101
Jordan's story on, 7, 100–101
LeVert's story on, 103–110
Louis's story on lack of, 95–97
mindset for, 81–84, 87–91
O'Neal's story on, 102
overview of, 7
personal sense of, 13–16, 82
racial disparities impacting, 96–97, 110
Robinson's story on, 101
socioeconomic status, wealth, and, 7, 81, 93–94, 97–102, 110–112, 114–115
venture capital for, 107–110
Williams's story on, 37–39, 101
Oxford University, 165

P

pandemic. *See* COVID-19 pandemic
Pappas, Art/Pappas Capital, 109
patents, 32–33, 128, 195–196
PepsiCo, 102
perceptions, 1, 9–13. *See also* mindset or mental attitude

pharmaceuticals. *See* Eli Lilly and Company
Philip Morris, 31–32
Pinky's Jamaican and American, 172
Piston Group, The, 101
Players Health, 129–130
politics
    DEI affected by, 5
    enclaves and, 51, 74–75
    innovation zone expansion support in, 193–194
    Louis influenced by, 96
    post-Civil War, 23
    racial disparities and, 1–2, 25–26, 96
    voting rights in, 69
Poro College, 20
post-overdose response (PORT) teams, 184–187
Powell, Adam Clayton, 54–55, 62
Powerful Noise, A, 112
PowerUp Initiative, 149, 151–154
Princeton University, 154–155
Procter and Gamble, 31–32, 33
Professional Development League, 190
professional diversity, 196
Prozac, 158
Purmal, Kate, 168

R

racial disparities. *See also* Black entrepreneurialism and innovation
- authors' experiences and perceptions of, 9–13
- economic loss due to, 4, 40–41
- in education, 65–66, 76, 103–104
- enclaves impacted by, 48–53, 56–58, 60–61, 63
- Great Migration due to, 49–50, 95
- in healthcare, 3, 37–38, 57–58, 124, 126–127, 136–137, 180–181
- impacts of, generally, 3–4
- innovation and entrepreneurship potential to transform, 2–3
- life expectancy and, 3
- mindset, attitudes, and, 56–57, 71–74, 81–82, 161–162
- ownership impacted by, 96–97, 110
- politics and, 1–2, 25–26, 96
- segregation and (*see* segregation)
- socioeconomic status and, 3–4, 22–23, 25–27
- systemic, 136–138
- venture capital and, 35–39, 137, 142, 146–147
- White supremacy and (*see* White supremacy)

Rebundle, 132
Redford, Robert, 112
Redhage, Chris, 191
religious institutions, 23, 54–55, 61–62, 76, 98
Retrace Health, 127
Reynolds, 45
Ricks, David, 158–160, 162, 170
ridesharing apps, 77–79
Rihanna (Robyn Rihanna Fenty), 110, 132–133
Road to Wigan Pier, The (Orwell), 9
Robert Wood Johnson Foundation, 60
Robinson, David, 101
Rocky Mount, North Carolina, 45–46, 50–53, 55–61, 63
Rocky Mount Event Center, 60
Rodgers, Johnathan, 74
Rondo neighborhood, 93–94
Ronnie Lott Foundation, 145
Roosevelt, Franklin Delano, 96

S

Sadgwar, Frederick, 25
Salamander Collection, 112
Salesforce, 149
San Antonio Spurs, 101
scalability
- challenges of, 6
- innovation zone expansion and, 174, 187
- proof of soundworthiness and, 32
- of Stewart's business, 79
- transformative change with, 6
- unique lenses leading to, 7, 121–123, 125, 127–128

Schering-Plough, 166
Schmeling, Max, 95–97
SchoolPool, LLC, 79
Schultz, Howard, 102
Second African Baptist Church (Savannah), 61
segregation
- in education, 65–66, 104, 115
- in enclaves, 51–52, 62

INDEX

history of Black entrepreneurialism and, 26–27, 40
Sendwave, 39
Serena Ventures, 37–39
Sherman, William Tecumseh, 61
Shuford Program in Entrepreneurship, 67, 75
Shukla, Shuchin, 179–183, 186–187
slave trade, 47. *See also* enslaved African Americans
Slutty Vegan, 173–174
Snoop Dogg, 173
Snowe, Olympia, 177
socioeconomic status. *See also* wealth
 disparities in, 3–4, 22–23, 26
 innovation and entrepreneurship improving, 5–6, 25–27
 innovation creating uncertainty for, 14–15
 ownership and, 81, 93–94, 97–102, 110–112
 racial disparities and, 3–4, 22–23, 25–27
 unique lenses for opportunity to better, 122
Somali immigrants, 176–179
Sonavi Labs, 128–129
South by Southwest, 140
Southeast TechInventures, 108
Spaulding, Charles Clinton, 29–30
Speight, Doug, 31–36, 43
Speight, Joye, 34–35
Speight, Melvin, 31
Speight, Theodore Roosevelt, 30–31
Spelman College, 117–118
sports. *See also specific athletes*
 education and, 54, 76, 104, 106, 129, 145

history of Black entrepreneurialism and, 36–37
 innovation zone expansion through, 190–194
 ownership lacking after success in, 95–97
 ownership path from, 98–102, 112, 192–193
 racial disparities in choice of, 72, 161–162
 startup for athlete support in, 107, 129–130
 unique lenses on, 129–132, 192
Stanford University, 108, 131, 145, 147, 154–155
Starbucks, 102
startups. *See also* Black entrepreneurialism and innovation
 enclaves supporting, 57, 73, 75, 77–79, 82–84, 89
 failure of, as valuable, 107
 healthcare, 125–126, 136, 140–141
 ownership of, 97, 99, 107–109, 111–112
 Speight family, 31–36
 statistics on, 3, 151
 support for, generally, 35–36
 transformative change with, 7–8, 136–137, 140–142, 144, 146
 unicorn, 3, 129
 unique lenses on opportunities for (*see* unique lenses)
 venture capital for, 36–39, 78, 123, 125–126, 137, 141–142 (*see also* venture capital)
 venture studio model, 144, 149–153, 182, 186
Stewart, Martha, 174

223

Stewart, Nehemiah, 75–80
stimulation of innovation, 157–170
    diversity underlying, 158–170
        Eli Lilly's efforts on, 8, 157–159, 162, 170
        overview of, 8, 157
St. Luke Emporium, 24
St. Luke's Penny Savings Bank, 23–25
Stradford, J. B./Stradford Hotel, 27
Sullivan, Leon, 53–56, 57, 62

Sum of Us: What Racism Costs Everyone and How We Can Prosper Together (McGhee), 40
SUNY, 108
support for innovation
    enclaves providing (*see* enclaves)
    financial (*see* loans and mortgages; venture capital)
    marginalized entrepreneurs receiving, 4–5
    transformative change with, 7–8, 135–155
Sweet Auburn Historic District, 62

T

Tavolo, 178
Taylor, Dasia, 126–127
Teal Health, 39
Techstars, 146, 178
Tennessee State University, 137
TerraLink, 122–123
Tesla, 116
Thomas, Ashlie, 117–123
tobacco, 45, 47, 50–52, 68
Tonal, 39
Totem, 188
transformative change, 135–155
    Eshelman Innovation's role in, 143–144, 149, 151–155
    Evans's role in, 144–149
    in healthcare, 136–141
    innovation acceleration models for, 142–149
    mindset for, 139, 148, 153, 155
    scalability for, 6
    with support for innovation, 7–8, 135–155
    systemic, 2–3
    trust building and, 153–155
    venture capital supporting, 137, 141–153, 193
    venture studio model for, 144, 149–153
    Whitney driving, 135–141
Trotman, Alex, 86
True Reformers Bank, 24
trust, building, 153–155
Tulane University, 180
Tulsa, Oklahoma, 27–29
Tuscarora people, 46–47
Tuskegee Institute, 116
TV One, 74–75
Twilio, 150
two-dimensional (2-D) diversity, 196
"Two Treatises of Government" (Locke), 13

U

Uber Eats, 173
unicorn startups, 3, 129
unique lenses, 113–133
    of Abuzeid, 129
    of Aderinkomi, 127–128
    on beauty industry, 132–133
    of Burkes, 129–130
    capitalizing on, 114–116
    of Carver, 115–116

INDEX

for community support, 120–123, 128–129, 131–132
diversity creating, 113–114, 117, 123, 128–129, 133
of Durrah, 123–124
on food and nutrition, 119–125
on healthcare, 125–129
of Hughes, 130–132
innovation zone expansion through, 174, 192
of May, 132
of Menker, 125
mindset for entrepreneurialism and, 122
overview of, 7, 113–114
of Rihanna, 132–133
scalability of ideas from, 7, 121–123, 125, 127–128
on sports and entertainment, 129–132, 192
of Taylor, 126–127
of Thomas, 117–123
venture capital to invest in, 113–114, 123, 125–126, 128–132
of West, 128–129
United Somali Women of Maine, 177
University of Arizona, 78
University of Bath, 10
University of Illinois, 111
University of Maryland, 76
University of North Carolina, Chapel Hill
Bell at, 67, 71, 72, 75, 78
Bernstein at, 59
Blackwell at, 55
Crowell as advisor to, 33
Eshelman Innovation at (*see* Eshelman Innovation)
Jordan at, 76, 100

Shuford Program in Entrepreneurship, 67, 75
Stewart at, 75–80
Thomas at, 117, 120–122
University of Tennessee, 34
USDA, 178
USL, 192
US News and World Report, 107

V

Vaughan, Sarah, 52
Vector Rideshare, 79
venture capital
diversity, equity, and inclusion in, 146–147
in history of Black entrepreneurialism, 35–39, 43
innovation zone expansion with, 174, 191–194
for ownership, 107–110
racial disparities and, 35–39, 137, 142, 146–147
for Stewart, 78–79
transformative change through, 137, 141–153, 193
for unique lens concepts, 113–114, 123, 125–126, 128–132
venture studio model, 144, 149–153, 182, 186
Viacom, 111
Voting Rights Act (1965), 69

W

Walgreens Boots Alliance, 166
Walker, Charles Joseph, 19, 20
Walker, Madam C. J., 17–22, 41, 62, 132
Walker, Maggie Lena, 23–25
Washington, Booker T., 116
Washington, George, 54

225

Washington Capitals, 112
Washington Mystics, 112
Washington Wizards, 101, 112
Watchmen, 28
Watts Uprising (1965), 124
Wayland Seminary, 54
wealth. *See also* socioeconomic status
    enclaves supporting opportunities for, 56–57
    generational, 4, 5, 86, 94, 101, 110, 114–115
    history of Black entrepreneurial, 18, 22, 26–27, 36–37
    innovation for growth of, 6, 42
    ownership generating, 7, 93–94, 98–102, 110–112, 114–115
    statistics on, 94
    transformative change in, 136–137, 142, 153
West, Ellington, 128–129
West, James, 128
West Virginia State College, 54
Wheaties, 100
White supremacy
    Great Migration due to, 49, 95
    healthcare foundations in, 136
    history of rise of, 26, 27–28
    in Lewiston, Maine, 176–177
    Louis's story on, 95, 96
Whitney, Marcus, 135–141, 190–193
Whole Foods, 124
Wiggins, Joel, 80–91
Williams, Serena, 36–39, 43, 101, 110
Wilmington, North Carolina, 25–26
Winfrey, Oprah, 110, 172
Woman's Journey, The (Eli Lilly), 159–160, 162, 168–169
women. *See also by name*
    corporate experiences of, 159–160, 162, 164–170
    economic loss from underrepresentation of, 41
    history of entrepreneurial, 17–22, 23–25, 36–39
    imposter syndrome among, 168, 170
    innovation zone expansion for, 171–175
    unique lenses of, 128–129
    venture capital for, 142, 146
Wonder, Stevie, 74
Woods, Tiger, 37, 101, 110

X
Xerox, 71

Y
Yale University, 54, 76
Y Combinator, 146

Z
Zwahlen, Roy, 10–11